LONDON ON A PLATE

First published 2002
by Black & White Publishing Ltd, Edinburgh EH6 6BZ
ISBN 1 902927 31 1

British Library Cataloguing in Publication data: a catalogue record for this
book is available from The British Library.

Design concept by Navy Blue

Printed and bound in Spain by Bookprint, S.L., Barcelona

LONDON ON A PLATE

PHOTOGRAPHS BY PAUL DODDS

BLACK & WHITE PUBLISHING

We have reproduced the recipes as supplied by the chefs, according to their own individual cooking styles. All recipes serve four, unless otherwise stated.

Contents

Weights, measures and servings

All weights, measures and servings are approximate conversions.

SOLID WEIGHT CONVERSIONS

Metric	Imperial
10g	$^1/_2$ oz
20g	$^3/_4$ oz
25g	1 oz
40g	$1^1/_2$ oz
50g	2 oz
60g	$2^1/_2$ oz
75g	3 oz
110g	4 oz
125g	$4^1/_2$ oz
150g	5 oz
175g	6 oz
200g	7 oz
225g	8 oz
250g	9 oz
275g	10 oz
350g	12 oz
450g	1 lb
700g	$1^1/_2$ lb
900g	2 lb
1.35kg	3 lb

STANDARDS SOLID

1 oz	=	25g
1 lb	=	16 oz
1 g	=	0.35 oz
1 kg	=	2.2 lb

LIQUID CONVERSIONS

Metric	Imperial
55ml	2 fl.oz
75ml	3 fl.oz
150ml	5 fl.oz ($^1/_4$ pint)
275ml	$^1/_2$ pint
425ml	$^3/_4$ pint
570ml	1 pint
725ml	$1^1/_4$ pints
1 litre	$1^3/_4$ pints
1.2 litre	2 pints
1.5 litre	$2^1/_2$ pints
2.25 litre	4 pints

STANDARDS LIQUID

1 tsp	=	5ml
1 tbsp	=	15ml
1 fl.oz	=	30ml
1 pint	=	20 fl.oz
1 litre	=	35 fl.oz

OVEN TEMPERATURE CONVERSIONS

°C	Gas	°F
140	1	275
150	2	300
170	3	325
180	4	350
190	5	375
200	6	400
220	7	425
230	8	450
240	9	475

Introduction

Can any single book ever do justice to the wealth of outstanding restaurants that crowd the streets of London? It is, after all, a city famed for its culinary excellence, the creativity of its chefs and the sheer diversity of food to be found here.

London on a Plate is your hors d'oeuvre – a tempting appetiser. The establishments featured allow you to sample the delights of London's cooking elite and go at least some way towards reflecting the range of cooking styles on offer. Some, like Antonio Carluccio and Brian Turner, are household names while others are from the new, young generation of chefs now taking the city by storm.

All, however, have been asked to reveal the secrets of four dishes – a starter, two main courses and a dessert – and the result is a sumptuous feast. Each chef brings you either their signature dishes or their personal favourites, and whether it is simple food that can be prepared in minutes, or more complex creations requiring detailed planning, the mouthwatering results will more than repay your efforts.

London on a Plate is a slice through the heart of London's cuisine, a snap-shot of the latest trends and styles, and a chance for you to see how differently ingredients can taste in the hands of different chefs. And if you're drawn in by the stunning images but can't face recreating them yourself, you can always book a table and allow the experts to entertain you.

Vineet Bhatia
Bar Zaika Bazaar

Vineet Bhatia
Bar Zaika Bazaar

I believe in following my heart. And I love food. I didn't so much choose cooking as feel myself being irresistibly drawn under its spell by its diversity and the opportunities it offers – the chance to express yourself and to work in an extremely creative environment.

I trained at The Oberoi Hotels in India, learning both the traditional methods and dishes but also developing my own style of cooking. I call this 'evolved Indian', lightening the traditional ghee-based curries whilst at the same time taking care to lift but not distort traditional concepts. I marry flavours from different regions of India and see no problem with this as long as it is done correctly and suits the dish. You see, it is important to me that I remain authentic in terms of the flavouring and use of spices. If you get your spicing right and present your food well on the plate, you're on to a winner.

I came to London in 1993 because it is a city packed with people who are as passionate about food as I am. I love the sheer variety on offer here and knew that it was the ideal place for me to develop my art. I launched Zaika in May 1999, where we create evolved Indian cuisine within calm, contemporary surroundings. And we were awarded a Michelin star in January 2001 for all our hard work – the first time an Indian restaurant has received such recognition. The following June I launched Bar Zaika Bazaar, a less formal sister restaurant serving chakna – simple Indian street food – along with drinks. Here we use only the best ingredients, executing each dish to exacting standards while keeping our food affordable. Those chosen here are some of my favourites – an Indian-style risotto, spicy sea bass and crusted lamb biryani, all rounded off with some chocolate – yes, chocolate! – samosas. Irresistible!

Gosht dum biryani

lamb biryani

300g baby lamb, diced (2.5cm)
80ml vegetable oil

for the marinade
1 tsp ground coriander seeds
2 tsp ground roasted spices (star anise, fennel seeds, green cardamom seeds and mace)
2 tbsp fresh mint, chopped
4 tbsp fressh coriander leaves, chopped
1 tbsp tomato paste
30g ghee or clarified butter (butter melted and strained through a cloth)
salt to taste

for the rice
500g basmati rice
1 pinch of turmeric powder
1 pinch of fennel seeds
3 star anise
6 green cardamom
1 blade of mace
1/2 onion, finely sliced and fried until crisp and brown
2 tbsp coriander leaves, chopped
2 tbsp mint leaves, chopped
a few drops of rose water (optional)

other ingredients
350g puff pastry, ready-made
15g melon seeds
15g fennel seeds
10g ground cardamom powder
50ml melted ghee

For the lamb: mix the lamb with the marinade and leave in the fridge overnight to infuse. Pour the oil into a pan and bring it up to a medium heat. Add the spiced meat, heat through to simmering point and cook for 1 hour, adding a little water from time to time to keep the meat moist and prevent it from burning. Put the meat to one side and keep it warm.

For the rice: pour about 3 litres of water into a pan, add all the spices used to flavour the rice and bring the water to a boil. Add the rice and cook until three-quarters done. Drain it off and keep it warm, mixing in the fried onion, coriander leaves and rose water.

To prepare the dish, preheat the oven to 200°C (gas mark 6). Fill either one large casserole or four individual bowls with alternating layers of rice and meat. Roll out the pastry into a circle to overlap the edge of the dish, seal the casserole with the pastry, stud the top with a few melon and fennel seeds, and sprinkle with ground cardamom powder. Bake in the oven for 20 minutes, and brush with the melted ghee or clarified butter. Serve at the table, cutting the pastry top in a wide circle to release the aroma.

Tikhi machli

spicy sea bass

4 x 200g sea bass fillets

for the marinade

3 cloves of garlic, chopped

6 long red chillies, blanched and puréed

60ml vegetable oil

salt to taste

juice of 1/2 lemon

for the sauce

120g yoghurt

20g gramflour

1/2 tsp turmeric powder

salt to taste

300ml water

50ml vegetable oil

1 tsp cumin seeds

1.25cm stem ginger julienne

1 green chilli julienne

1 red chilli, whole

1 sprig of curry leaves

1 pinch of asafoetida (optional)

2 tbsp coriander leaves, chopped

for the couscous

15ml vegetable oil

15g unsalted butter

1 tsp mustard seeds

1 tsp fresh ginger, chopped

1 tsp green chilli, chopped

1 sprig of curry leaves

75g coarse semolina

240ml warm water

80ml coconut milk

1 tsp lemon juice

salt to taste

1 tsp caster sugar

2 tbsp coriander leaves, chopped

for the garnish

mango julienne

Fillet, scale, pin-bone and trim the fish. Cut each fillet into half and make gashes on the skin. Mix together the marinade ingredients, rub them over the fish and refrigerate for 30 minutes.

For the sauce: mix together the yoghurt, gramflour, turmeric, salt and water. Heat the oil in a pot and add the cumin seeds, ginger julienne, green chilli julienne, whole red chilli, curry leaves and asafoetida in quick succession. As the mixture splutters, add the yoghurt mixture and bring to a boil. Reduce the heat and simmer for 8 minutes, stirring continuously to avoid lumps forming. Strain the sauce, adding a little water if required, and lastly add the chopped coriander leaves and check the seasoning.

For the couscous: heat up a deep pan, and add the oil and butter. Add the mustard seeds and, as they crackle, add the ginger, green chilli and curry leaves. Lower the heat and add the semolina, dry-roasting for 5–6 minutes until it releases a nutty aroma. Stir in the warm water and coconut milk, increase the heat and add the lemon juice, salt and sugar, cooking for a further 3 minutes. Lastly add the coriander leaves before serving.

To prepare the dish, cook the marinated fish in a non-stick pan for 4 minutes, placing the fish skin-side down. Turn the fish when the skin crispens and is half cooked, and cook for a further 1 minute. Allow it to rest for a couple of minutes before serving. Spoon the couscous on to the centre of a large soup plate. Pour the sauce around it and place the pan-fried sea bass on top. Garnish with raw mango julienne.

Jhinga khichdi

Indian risotto

for the prawns

2 eggs

1 tsp fresh coriander, chopped

1/2 tsp red chilli powder

salt to taste

1 tbsp cornflour

8 medium-sized prawns, deveined

vegetable oil for deep-frying

for the rice

40ml vegetable oil

1 tsp cumin seeds

3 cloves of garlic, chopped

1 tbsp fresh ginger, chopped

1 tbsp green chilli, chopped

1 red onion, peeled and chopped

1 tsp turmeric powder

250g basmati rice

625ml shellfish stock (use ground lobster, langoustine and prawn shells)

4 tbsp plain yoghurt, whipped

1 tbsp unsalted butter

1 tbsp fresh coriander, chopped

1 tbsp salt, to taste

For the prawns: beat the eggs, coriander, chilli powder, salt and cornflour into a batter. Coat the prawns, deep-fry them for 30 seconds–1 minute and drain. Keep them on one side until needed.

For the rice: heat the oil to a medium heat and add the cumin until it splutters. Add the garlic and sauté for a minute, then add the ginger, chilli and onion, and sauté for 2 minutes. Add the turmeric and rice and beat for 2 minutes. Pour in the warmed stock, bring it to the boil, then reduce the heat and cook for 15 minutes until the rice is three-quarters done and the stock absorbed. Add the yoghurt and continue cooking until the rice is ready, stirring in the butter and coriander to finish and seasoning to taste. To prepare the dish, reheat the prawns, serving them on top of the rice.

Vineet Bhatia
Bar Zaika Bazaar

Chocomosa

chocolate samosas with cardamom ice-cream

60g almond slivers
200ml double cream
200ml milk
juice of $1/4$ lemon
200g white chocolate
200g plain chocolate
15g plain flour
30ml water
16 samosa pads
vegetable oil for deep-frying
cardamom ice-cream
4 sprigs of mint to garnish

Preheat the oven to 140°C (gas mark 1) and roast the almond slivers for 1–2 minutes until golden. Allow them to cool. Bring the cream and milk to the boil and add the lemon juice to curdle the mixture. Strain it through a muslin cloth and squeeze out any excess liquid. Melt the chocolates in 2 separate bain-maries and reserve 30g of each for decoration in piping bags. Divide the split milk mixture into two, add the almonds to both, with the white chocolate in one half and the plain chocolate in the other.

Make a slurry of plain flour and water. Stuff the two chocolate mixtures separately into each samosa pad, and seal with the flour slurry. Heat up the vegetable oil and deep-fry the samosas for 30 seconds or until golden brown.

Serve with cardamom ice-cream and top with a sprig of mint.

Guy Bossom
The People's Palace

Guy Bossom
The People's Palace

I like to think that I have a balanced approach to life, organising things carefully and never getting carried away by events. But one event did take me by surprise. Never for one moment did I imagine that a summer job when I was thirteen would develop into such an exciting career.

The job in question was – predictably enough – in a restaurant. And just a few short years later I found myself working in Michelin-starred establishments like Relais à Bracieux in the Loire Valley and Chez Nico in Park Lane – both of which had two stars at the time. Indeed, Nico Ladenis' simple, common-sense approach to cooking has helped to shape my whole philosophy of food and, in a way, this is reflected in the dishes we prepare at The People's Palace.

Here we want our guests to understand the food that they're eating. We always make sure that there is plenty to choose from and that the weekends become child-friendly, family occasions. For all its buzz, however, the large dining room is light and airy and has wonderful views over the river, giving it an inviting but uncluttered feel. The recipes that follow are favourites at The People's Palace, modern British dishes with an eclectic twist that I hope you enjoy.

Grilled red mullet

with mangetout and tomato and olive oil dressing

for the tomato and olive oil dressing

100g fresh plum tomatoes, roughly chopped
50ml extra virgin olive oil
1 clove of garlic
2 large basil leaves, torn
salt and black pepper

for the rouille

50g potato (mashing)
1 hard-boiled egg, yolk only
20g red chilli, finely chopped and deseeded
2 cloves of garlic, crushed
1 small pinch of saffron stamens, soaked in 50ml tepid water
40ml pasteurised egg yolks
250ml Olivetti oil (mild olive oil)
salt and black pepper
juice of 1 lemon

for the salsa verde

1 clove of garlic
25g fresh flat-leaf parsley
10g fresh mint
25g fresh basil
10g fine capers
10g Dijon mustard
10ml white wine vinegar
60ml extra virgin olive oil
salt and black pepper

for the mullet

8 x 50g red mullet fillets, scaled and pin-boned
olive oil
salt and black pepper

other ingredients

120g mangetout, topped, tailed and cut into thin strips
20ml walnut oil
1 slice of white bread
60g frisé lettuce, picked and washed
4 sprigs of fresh chervil, picked, to garnish

For the tomato and olive oil dressing: put all the ingredients into a tall container and cover the mixture with clingfilm. Allow it to sit for approximately 1 hour so that the flavours can infuse, liquidise it, check the seasoning and serve as required.

For the rouille: boil the potatoes in salted water and drain them well. Then crush them in a bowl with the hard-boiled egg yolk, chilli, garlic and saffron until well mixed. Add the pasteurised egg yolk, mix well again, and slowly add the oil as if making mayonnaise, mixing it in quickly and thoroughly as you go so as not to split the mixture. Season with salt, pepper and lemon juice to taste, and serve as required.

For the salsa verde: blend all the ingredients together in a food processor for approximately 20–30 seconds, season and serve as required. (If it is too thick, adjust with a little water then blend again. You should be able to drizzle this around the dish.)

For the mullet: place the red mullets on a suitable baking tray, skin-side up. Rub with olive oil and seasoning and place them under a hot grill for about 2 minutes until the skin is crispy and the fish are just cooked.

To prepare the dish, sauté the mangetout in the walnut oil for about 2 minutes until it starts to wilt, season it and remove it from the heat. Cut the bread into 4 round croûtons and fry them in olive oil until golden. Then place a small pile of the cooked mangetout on the plate and top it with one of the fish fillets. Place more mangetout and frisé lettuce on top of this, and place the second fillet on top of this. More mangetout and lettuce go on top, and then spoon some rouille on to the croûton and place this on the top. Drizzle some of the tomato and olive oil dressing and salsa verde around, garnish with a sprig of chervil and serve.

Pan-fried skate wing

with golden sultana, beetroot and caper butter

for the red wine fish jus

200g lemon sole bones, soaked in cold water and drained (blood and gills removed)

30ml vegetable oil

100ml red wine

300ml veal stock

60ml ruby port

1g herbes de Provence, dried

salt and black pepper

for the potatoes

100g unsalted butter

200g ratte potatoes (French elongated new potatoes), peeled and one edge cut flat

salt and black pepper

for the skate

4 x 250g skate wings, trimmed

40ml vegetable oil

100g unsalted butter, diced

1 whole lemon, cut in half, for juice

25g golden sultanas, soaked in tepid water for 1 hour until plump

80g cooked beetroot, peeled and cut into wedges

20g extra fine capers

10g fresh flat-leaf parsley, finely shredded

80g watercress

For the red wine fish jus: chop the fish bones into 5cm pieces, sweat them in vegetable oil quickly in a saucepan to give a little colour, add the red wine and reduce to a syrup. Add the veal stock, cook for 20 minutes and reduce to a thick jus. Add the ruby port and cook for 5 minutes more until a thick syrup is achieved. Remove this from the heat, add the herbes de Provence and allow them to infuse for 10 minutes. Pass the jus through a chinois, then a double muslin cloth, check the seasoning and pour it into a squeezy bottle for serving.

For the potatoes: slice the butter and lay the slices over the bottom of a cold medium-sized frying pan. Lay the ratte potatoes, flat-side down, on top of the butter. Just cover them with cold water, place the frying pan over a full gas flame and allow it to boil rapidly until all the water has evaporated. At this point, turn the flame down low and cook the potatoes until golden brown. Remove the potatoes from the butter and season.

For the skate wings: preheat the oven to 220°C (gas mark 7). Sauté the skate wings in vegetable oil in a hot pan for 2 minutes either side or until dark golden, remove them from the pan on to a tray and finish cooking them in the oven for about 1 1/2 minutes.

For the butter: add the diced butter to the hot pan used to sauté the skate and cook it to noisette (a deep-brown colour). Arrest the browning of the butter with the lemon juice, remove it from the heat and add the sultanas, beetroot, capers and julienne of flat parsley.

To prepare the dish, reheat the fondant potatoes in the oven at 220°C (gas mark 7) for 1 1/2 minutes. Place the skate wing in the middle of the plate on top of the watercress with two fondant potatoes on top. Drizzle a thread of the red wine fish jus around, then spoon the noisette butter over the skate wing and serve.

Loin of lamb
with Merguez, roast tomato and garlic jus

1 whole short lamb saddle, on-the-bone (bone out loins, keep bones for sauce, keep kidneys for dish)

for the persillage
25g fresh rosemary
100g fresh parsley
100g white breadcrumbs, dried
10g garlic
20g clarified butter
salt and black pepper

for the tomatoes
2 plum tomatoes, halved

for the garlic lamb jus
500g lamb bones, chopped small and roasted until brown
100g carrots, roughly chopped
100g onions, roughly chopped
400ml vegetable oil
200ml dry white wine
1 litre veal stock
500ml cold water
100ml tomato juice
100g leeks, chopped
1 stick of celery
20g fresh rosemary
100g tomatoes
50g garlic, crushed
knob of butter
30g roasted garlic, removed from its skin and puréed

for the lamb
30g egg white, broken with fork, not whisked
knob of butter

other ingredients
olive oil
4 Merguez sausages
salt and black pepper
4 medium courgettes, each cut into 3 lengthways
12 cloves of garlic, roasted in their skin in 30g duck fat
12 baby onions, peeled and roasted in 30g duck fat

For the persillage: in a food blender, blend all the ingredients together very briefly. It should have the appearance of moist green breadcrumbs, not a dough. Taste, season and put on one side until required.

For the tomatoes: preheat the oven to 100°C. Put the halves of tomato into the oven for 2–3 hours, until they have reduced in size by around a half but have not coloured. These can be done in advance if necessary.

For the garlic lamb jus: when the lamb bones are roasted, drain them in a colander. In a thick-bottomed pan, sauté the carrots and onions in vegetable oil until a good brown colour. Stir them well and drain them. Return the carrots, onions and lamb bones to the pan, bring them back to the heat, deglaze with the white wine and reduce the wine to a syrup. Add the veal stock, water, tomato juice and the remaining vegetables and herbs, apart from the roasted garlic purée, and bring the mixture back to the boil, simmering slowly and skimming constantly for 1–1½ hours. Pass through a seive and then a muslin cloth, discarding the bones and vegetables. Bring back to the boil and reduce to the desired sauce consistency, whilst skimming frequently. Pass through a muslin cloth once more, then refrigerate until needed.

For the lamb: cut the lamb saddle loins across the centre to give you 4 140g portions. Roll them in the egg white and then in the persillage, and store them on baking paper in the fridge, not touching each other. Preheat the oven to 150°C (gas mark 2). When needed, seal the coated lamb in a knob of butter and place them in the oven. Do not colour them too much (turn them after 2 minutes and remove them after 2 more), then allow them to rest out of the oven for 5 minutes before serving.

To prepare the dish, sauté the lamb kidneys in a little vegetable oil until just pink inside, season and allow them to rest for 3 minutes. Sauté the courgette slices quickly in a little vegetable oil in another pan until golden brown but still slightly crispy. Sauté the Merguez sausages in a little vegetable oil for 4–5 minutes until cooked, then allow them to rest for 3 minutes. Heat the jus, whisk in a knob of butter and the roasted garlic purée and check the seasoning. Reheat the rest of the garnishes in a hot oven (220°C) for approximately 2 minutes. Arrange the garnish in the centre of the dish with the courgette slices laid in a triangle and the roasted tomato, kidney and garlic on top. Cut the rested hot lamb across into 3 equal pieces and arrange it around the outside of the garnish, putting the Merguez and baby onions in between. Spoon the sauce around and serve.

Pink grapefruit and lime bavarois

with basil syrup

for the Genoise sponge
300ml whole eggs
90g caster sugar
90g flour

for the basil syrup
120ml stock syrup
100g red basil, leaves and stalks

for the bavarois
150g double cream
1 egg yolk
30g caster sugar
185g pink grapefruit purée, bought
or made by blending grapefruit
segments in a blender
2 leaves of gelatine, soaked
zest and juice of 1 lime
8 pink grapefruit segments
4 white grapefruit segments
4 sprigs of mint

For the Genoise sponge: preheat the oven to 180°C (gas mark 4). Cream the eggs and sugar together for about 10 minutes until light and white. Add the flour, mix it in well, then spread the mixture on to lightly buttered silicon/baking paper on a baking tray so it is about 1/2 cm thick. Cook it in the oven for 9 minutes, then remove it, allow to cool slightly and wrap it in clingfilm until required.

For the basil syrup: warm the syrup, add the basil leaves, liquidise the mixture then pass it through a muslin cloth and chill.

For the bavarois: whisk the double cream to stiff peaks and set it aside. Mix the egg yolk, lime zest and sugar over a bain-marie until it is a thick and light sabayon, then remove this from the heat. Bring half the grapefruit purée to the boil, add the gelatine leaves and allow them to dissolve. Mix this with the other half of the pink grapefruit purée and lime juice, then thoroughly mix together the cream, sabayon and grapefruit purée. Place baking paper on a tray with a 20 x 12cm rectangular mould (or individual moulds, if you prefer) on top. Line the bottom of the mould with the Genoise sponge, top it with the bavarois mixture and place this in the fridge to set (preferably overnight).

To prepare the dish, drizzle the basil syrup on to the serving dish, cut the bavarois with a hot knife into portion sizes and place the bavarois just off centre. Arrange 2 pink grapefruit and 1 white grapefruit segments next to the bavarois on each plate and top with a sprig of mint or basil if you prefer. You can serve a light biscuit with this dish to give it a different texture.

John Burton-Race

The John Burton-Race Restaurant at
The Landmark Hotel

John Burton-Race
The John Burton-Race Restaurant at
The Landmark Hotel

If I told the story of how I became a chef, we'd be here all night! Suffice it to say that one thing led to another and my commitment to achieving the highest possible standards in everything I do eventually brought me to the job of Sous Chef at the celebrated Le Manoir aux Quat' Saisons. I then stayed with Raymond Blanc's team and became Head Chef/Manager at Le Petit Blanc in Oxford, before becoming Head Chef/Managing Director at L'Ortolan in Shinfield.

It is two Frenchman who have had the greatest influence in my cooking – Raymond Blanc and Gerard Boyer – so it is perhaps not surprising that French *haute cuisine* is what we are renowned for here at The John Burton-Race Restaurant. I started working in these grand and opulent surroundings in May 2000. I am extremely proud of retaining our two Michelin stars, and admit that my ambition is to win three (as well as to make loads of money, of course!). My favourite food? Unquestionably fish, shellfish and quality chocolate desserts – not to mention good strong coffee. But here I have selected turbot, scallops, beef with snails, and a raspberry assiette – which are current specialities on my à la carte menu.

Tian of turbot

with scallop mousse, thinly sliced scallops and truffle
essence

for the fish stock

2 shallots, finely chopped

1 sprig of fresh thyme

1/2 fresh bay leaf

1/2 clove of garlic, crushed

10ml olive oil

75ml Noilly Prat

100ml dry white wine

1kg fish bones

1 litre water

for the Madeira sauce

250g duck bones

50g mirepoix

1 sprig fresh thyme

1 clove of garlic, crushed

1/2 fresh bay leaf

10 ml mixed olive oil

10ml xeres vinegar

1/2 tbsp redcurrant jelly

20ml dry white wine

35ml Madeira

250ml chicken stock

10ml veal glace (not essential)

for the chicken jus

1.2kg chicken winglets

35ml olive oil

20g carrots

20g leeks

140g large onions

25g celery

1 clove of garlic

1 sprig of fresh thyme

1 fresh bay leaf

100ml dry white wine

2 litres water

for the turbot sauce

2 shallots, peeled and sliced

10ml olive oil

The fish stock, Madeira sauce and chicken jus need to be made in advance as they are needed later in the dish.

For the fish stock: in a large pan, sweat down the shallots, thyme, bay leaf and garlic in the olive oil. Add the Noilly Prat and reduce until almost dry, then add the white wine and reduce by half. At this stage you can store as 'mise en place' or continue to make the fish stock. Prepare the fish bones by removing the roe, innards or any dark skin from them, and running them under cold water for at least 2 hours (the longer the better). Add the bones to the shallot mixture and add the water. Bring the stock up to the boil and skim off any impurities while it simmers for 30 minutes. Allow the stock to cool down and then pass it through a fine chinois.

For the Madeira sauce: roast the bones in oil in the oven until they are golden brown. In a separate pan, lightly caramelise the mirepoix, thyme, garlic and bay leaf in olive oil. Add the xeres vinegar and reduce until completely dry. Add the roasted duck bones and redcurrant jelly and continue to caramelise, before adding the white wine and once again reducing until dry. Add the Madeira and reduce by seven-eighths, then cover the bones with chicken stock and simmer for approximately 2 hours. Pass the stock through a fine chinois, add the veal glace and reduce the stock to a sauce consistency. Pass the sauce through a fine chinois and set aside until needed.

For the chicken jus: chop the chicken winglets into 3 pieces and chop the vegetables into a large mirepoix. Heat up a roasting tray and roast the winglets in the olive oil until golden brown. Deglaze the tray with 1/2 litre of water and add the sediment to a large pan. In a separate pan, sauté the vegetables in a little olive oil until lightly coloured, add the herbs and white wine and reduce by two-thirds. Add the vegetable mixture to the pan with the chicken winglets and cover with water. Simmer for 2 hours and pass the stock through a fine chinois.

For the turbot sauce: sweat down the sliced shallots in the olive oil, add the Madeira and reduce by seven-eighths. Add the fish stock, Madeira sauce and chicken jus and simmer for 1 hour. Pass the stock through a fine chinois, reduce it by half, and finish by adding the truffle bouillon, chopped truffle and lemon juice.

For the turbot mousse: blend together the turbot and scallop trimmings with a little salt until smooth. Pass the puréed fish through a fine drum sieve and refrigerate it until it is very cold. Return the fish purée to the blender, mix in the egg yolk and gradually add the cream. At this stage

300ml Madeira
120ml fish stock
30ml Madeira sauce
280ml chicken jus
10ml truffle bouillon (optional)
1g chopped truffle
juice of 1/2 lemon

for the turbot mousse
45g turbot trimmings
70g scallop trimmings
salt
1 egg yolk
50ml whipping cream
cayenne pepper
squeeze of lemon juice

for the tian of turbot
4 x 80g discs of turbot, 6.5cm
diameter
1 courgette, thickly sliced into 4
and blanched
4 large scallops (dived), each finely
sliced into about 6 pieces
100ml fish stock

for the garnish
300ml fish stock
30g unsalted butter
12 new potatoes, peeled
12 baby leeks, trimmed
12 asparagus spears
4 slices of truffle
4 sprigs of chervil

do not over-blend the mix. Correct the seasoning, add lemon juice to taste and cook a little tester. Take a small amount of mousse, drop it into a small pan with water (enough to cover the top of the tester mousse) and poach for 3 minutes to make sure the mousse is the correct texture and flavour.

For tian of turbot: lightly butter four 6.5cm ring moulds. Place the turbot discs in the bottom with the courgette slices around sides. Pipe in the mousse filling to the top of the courgette band, and lay a fan of scallop discs, overlapping each other around the tian of the turbot. Preheat the oven to 200°C (gas mark 6). Bring 100ml of your fish stock up to the boil in a large pan and place the tians on top in a bain-marie style. Cover with a lid and cook in the oven for about 12 minutes. Remove the tians from the stock and allow them to rest for about 5 minutes before serving. Meanwhile, reduce the stock then add the other sauces.

To prepare the dish, add 100ml fish stock and 10g butter to each of 3 separate pans. Add the potatoes, baby leeks and asparagus into the 3 pans, gently heat up the garnish and reduce the stock down so it glazes the vegetables.

To serve, place the turbot tian in the middle of the dish. Garnish the dish with the glazed vegetables, a slice of truffle and a sprig of chervil, then pour the turbot sauce around the edge.

for the tarragon dressing
50ml olive oil
50ml arachide oil
1/4 clove of garlic
1 sprig of tarragon
10ml white wine vinegar

for the olive oil dressing
50ml olive oil
50ml arachide oil
juice of 1 lemon
1/2 clove of garlic, sliced

for the brunoise of vegetables
1 red pepper
1 yellow pepper
1 bulb of fennel
1 courgette
1 carrot

for the scallops
12 large scallops, thinly sliced
10ml olive oil
lemon juice

for the tomato coulis
3 plum tomatoes, halved and deseeded
10ml olive oil
2ml white wine vinegar
salt, sugar and white pepper

for the fish sauce
400ml fish stock
1/4 clove of garlic, sliced
50ml tarragon dressing
10g shallots, peeled and diced
lemon juice

for the salad
50g roquette
50g winter endive
1 shallot, peeled and diced
1/2 bunch of chives, finely chopped
salt and black pepper

for the garnish
1 tomato
3 black olives, pitted
20 sprigs of chervil

Thinly sliced marinated scallops

with crunchy vegetables, tomato coulis and a warm fish sauce

For the tarragon dressing: this dressing will give you a better result if it is made one day in advance. Whisk all the ingredients together, season to taste and set aside until required.

For the olive oil dressing: mix all the ingredients together and season to taste. This dressing should be kept in the fridge for a better result.

For the brunoise of vegetables: peel and cut the peppers and fennel bulb into a 1/2cm dice. Cut the courgette into quarters lengthways and remove most of the inside flesh, leaving the green skin and 1/2cm of the courgette. Then cut it into a 1/2cm dice like the peppers and fennel. Peel the carrot and cut it the same size as the courgette.

For the carpaccio of scallop: rub each slice of scallop with a little olive oil, season with salt and pepper and add a tiny drop of lemon juice to each.

For the tomato coulis: blitz the tomatoes until smooth, then pass them through a fine chinois before allowing them to drip through a muslin cloth for several hours. Once the water content has separated from the tomatoes, place the pulp in a bowl and whisk in the vinegar and olive oil until it emulsifies. Correct the seasoning with the salt, pepper and sugar.

For the fish sauce: reduce the fish stock and garlic in a pan until it forms a glace. Whisk in the tarragon dressing and add the diced shallots, keeping it warm until needed.

For the garnish: prepare the tomato by blanching it for 5 seconds in boiling water and refreshing it in iced water until cool. Remove the skin, deseed the flesh and cut it into diamond shapes – you need 5 per plate. Cut the olives in half and each half into 3 slices – you need 5 per plate.

To prepare the dish, mix the diced vegetables with the olive oil dressing and season to taste. Lay them in a ring around the plate and place the marinated scallops over the top. Pour the tomato coulis into the inner part of the circle, placing the tomato diamonds and black olives neatly around the plate. Mix the salad leaves with the diced shallot and chives, dress it with the tarragon dressing and season. Arrange this in the middle of the ring on top of the tomato coulis. To finish the dish, pour the warm fish sauce around the plate and over the scallops and place the chervil on top of the black olives before serving.

Roasted fillet of beef

with snails rolled in parsley garlic butter and red wine sauce

for the veal glace

6kg veal bones

300g mirepoix (equal proportions of carrot, onion, leek, celery, cut large)

20ml olive oil

10g tomato purée

100g tomatoes, squeezed

4 cloves of garlic

1/2 fresh bay leaf

1 sprig of thyme

150ml Madeira

200g button mushrooms

for the onion purée

200g onions

1 sprig of thyme

1/2 fresh bay leaf

3 cloves of garlic, crushed

40g unsalted butter

60ml chicken stock

100ml double cream

salt and white pepper

for the parsley butter

1 bunch of flat-leaf parsley

1/2 clove of garlic, crushed

125g unsalted butter

salt and white pepper

for the court bouillon

250g onions, finely diced

100g carrots, finely diced

150g leeks, finely diced

10g fennel, finely diced

5g garlic, crushed

10ml olive oil

50ml white wine vinegar

dry white wine

1 litre water

1 fresh bay leaf

For the veal glace: roast the veal bones in the oven on a tray without any oil until they are all golden brown. In a large stockpot add the mirepoix and olive oil and caramelise the vegetables until they are all lightly golden. Add the tomato purée, squeezed tomatoes, garlic cloves, bay leaves and thyme, then the roasted veal bones and cover with water. Simmer the veal stock for approximately 6 to 8 hours, pass it through a fine chinois and refrigerate. When required, remove the fat from the set stock, warm it in a pan and reduce it by half. Add the Madeira and sliced button mushrooms, reduce the stock by a further three-quarters of its original volume and then set aside until needed.

For the onion purée: in a large pan slowly sweat the onions, thyme, bay leaf and garlic with the butter until they are soft. Strain off the onions, remove the herbs and reduce the remaining liquid by three-quarters of its original volume, then add to the chicken stock and cream. In another pan simmer together the chicken stock and cream for approximately 45 minutes. Blend together the onions and cream in a liquidiser until smooth and pass the purée through a fine chinois. Correct the seasoning and set aside until needed.

For the parsley butter: blanch the parsley in boiling salted water and refresh in iced water. Set up the liquidiser and blend the parsley and garlic into a smooth purée. Then, either blitz the butter or stir it using a wooden spoon until it is smooth. Add the parsley purée and continue to blend. Season with salt and pepper, roll the parsley butter in clingfilm and store it in the freezer until needed.

For the court bouillon: sweat down the diced vegetables and crushed garlic in the olive oil in a large pan. Add the white wine vinegar, reduce the mixture by three-quarters, then add the white wine and reduce by half. Add the water, herbs, salt, peppercorns and star anise, bring it up to the boil then remove from the heat and leave to cool until needed.

For the snails: place the snails into a container and sprinkle the sea salt all over them. This process will extract any impurities and purify them. Rinse the snails under cold water for at least 1 hour to remove any unwanted residue that remains. Place the washed snails into the court bouillon, and simmer gently for approximately 1 hour.

For the red wine sauce: sweat the shallots, thyme, garlic and bay leaf in the olive oil in a large pan. Add the red wine vinegar and reduce until completely dry. Then add the port and reduce once more to a syrupy consistency. Add the red wine and button mushrooms, and reduce by

1 sprig of thyme

2 parsley stalks

75g salt

4g peppercorns

1 star anise

for the snails

100g fresh snails

100g coarse sea salt

500ml court bouillon

for the red wine sauce

40ml olive oil

150g shallots, peeled and chopped

1 sprig of thyme

1 clove of garlic, peeled and
chopped

1 bay leaf

100ml red wine vinegar

300ml port

600ml red wine

100g button mushrooms, sliced

4 litres chicken stock

40ml veal glace

for the garnish

60g girolle mushrooms

40g unsalted butter

¹/₄ clove of garlic, crushed

120g button onions

2 large potatoes, peeled and cut
into thin strips

40g clarified butter

for the beef fillet

4 x 150g portions of beef fillet

salt and black pepper

1 tsp olive oil

20g unsalted butter

20ml veal glace

two-thirds, before adding the chicken stock and veal glace and simmering for about 2 hours. Strain the stock through a fine chinois and reduce it until it reaches a sauce consistency. This should make 1 litre. When the sauce is finished, a reduction of port or red wine can be added to freshen the sauce.

For the garnish: sauté the girolles in one half of the butter with the garlic until they have softened, and sauté the button onions in the other half. In a non-stick pan, shape the potato strips into small galettes and slowly fry them in clarified butter until golden brown.

For the beef: preheat the oven to 210°C (gas mark 7). Season the beef fillets with salt and pepper. Add the olive oil to a hot pan and colour the beef on each side until golden brown. Then cook the beef in the oven for 3 minutes on each side, and rest it for a few minutes on one side. Remove the beef fillet from the pan and reduce the juices with the butter and veal glace to form a sticky glaze. Roll the beef fillet in this.

To prepare the dish, roll the snails in the parsley butter and warm them through gently. Warm the onion purée and place some in the middle of the plate with the glazed beef on top. Lay the snails, caramelised onions and girolles around the outside, pour the red wine sauce over them, topping the beef with the potato galette.

Assiette framboise

for the raspberry coulis
50g fresh raspberries
icing sugar

for the raspberry sorbet
200g fresh raspberries
215g stock syrup
65g water
200g dark chocolate
65g white chocolate

for the white chocolate mousse
160g white chocolate
10g icing sugar
10g egg yolk
50g whipping cream
1/4 leaf gelatine
100g double cream
20 raspberries
50ml raspberry coulis
4 sprigs of mint

for the pastry cream
250ml milk
3 egg yolks
50g caster sugar
25g plain flour

for the raspberry soufflé
50g unsalted butter, softened
4 egg whites
100g caster sugar
12 raspberries, soaked in eau de vie
10ml eau de vie (clear raspberry alcohol)

For the raspberry coulis: purée the fruit with the icing sugar and pass it through a fine sieve to remove the seeds. Leave on one side until needed.

For the raspberry sorbet: purée the raspberries in a blender with 50ml stock syrup and pass this through a fine sieve. Then mix this with the remaining stock syrup and water, and place it in a sorbet machine, churning until smooth. Freeze for one hour. Shape the raspberry sorbet into golf-ball sizes, melt the dark chocolate in a bain-marie, and dip the sorbet balls in. Reset them in the freezer, then melt the white chocolate, and stripe the outsides with it, keeping them in the freezer until required.

For the white chocolate mousse: melt 60g of the white chocolate in a bain-marie. Whisk the icing sugar with the egg yolks and add this to the melted chocolate. Boil 50g double cream, take it off the heat and dissolve the gelatine in it. Mix the double cream mixture with the melted chocolate and blend them until they are smooth and resemble a ganache consistency. Allow to cool before folding in the lightly whipped cream. Pour the white chocolate mousse into 4.5cm ring moulds and allow them to set in the fridge for approximately 4 hours. Melt the remaining white chocolate as above, spread it on to acetate and wrap it around the mousses. Allow them to set in the fridge for one further hour, keeping the mousses in the ring moulds. Remove them and gently peel off the acetate.

For the pastry cream: heat up the milk in a small pan. In a medium-size bowl, whisk the egg yolks and caster sugar together. Add the flour, continue to whisk, then pour the hot milk over the mixture, stirring continuously. Place the mixture back into the small pan and bring it up to the boil. Simmer for about 5 minutes, stirring continuously to stop it burning. Pour out on to a tray to cool.

For the soufflé: brush four 7cm ramekins with the soft butter and chill them in the fridge. Preheat the oven to 200°C (gas mark 7). Whisk the egg whites and caster sugar together to form firm peaks. In a large bowl whisk the cooled pastry cream and soaked raspberries until smooth. Whisk a quarter of the egg whites into the pastry mix until smooth, then fold in the other three-quarters to form a light airy soufflé mixture. Place this in the ramekins and cook for about 5 minutes in the oven, until they have risen about 4cm above the top of the moulds and are just coloured. To serve, remove the white chocolate mousse from the freezer. Place the raspberries in a bowl and mix them with the coulis. Arrange the glazed raspberries on top of the mousse and finish by topping with a sprig of mint. Place on a plate with the soufflé and sorbet ball and serve.

Antonio Carluccio
The Neal Street Restaurant

Antonio Carluccio
The Neal Street Restaurant

My mother inspired me to become a chef. She used the freshest ingredients to create classic Italian dishes that quite literally made my mouth water. This grounding in the basic techniques of cookery has stood me in good stead over the years.

I am open to new ideas but to this day remain a traditionalist at heart – a fact that has had a profound influence on the whole ethos of The Neal Street Restaurant. With no formal training (I started out as a wine seller in Vienna before moving to London), I worked in various places before taking over from Terence Conran here in 1981. And it is a restaurant that has allowed me to indulge in my passion – the vast array of styles and tastes that make up Italian regional cookery. This is our speciality – food that has simple, strong flavours that are uniquely Italian, like the Insalata di funghi misti, Lamb medallions with morels, Roman-style eel and Cioccolato cioccolato that I have chosen for the pages that follow.

We were voted Best Regional Italian Restaurant in Europe by the Accademia Italiana Della Cucina – an award I am justifiably proud of. But, when everyone in the UK knows our name and thinks of us as the epitome of fine Italian cooking, I know I will have done my job.

Insalata di funghi misti

500g mixed wild mushrooms
(cleaned weight)
8 tbsp extra virgin olive oil
1 clove of garlic, finely chopped
salt
1 tbsp parsley, finely chopped
8 slices of bread, toasted

Carefully clean the mushrooms and cut the larger ones in half. Put them into a pan with the olive oil and fry them gently. Add the garlic and fry for another 2–3 minutes. Add salt to taste, along with the parsley, and serve hot, with the toast on the side.

Roman-style eel

600g fresh eel, cut into 7¹/₂cm chunks
15 tbsp olive oil
salt and freshly ground black pepper
3 tbsp vinegar
2 tbsp fresh mint leave, finely chopped
400g green beans
3 cloves of garlic, finely chopped

Preheat the oven to 220°C (gas mark 7). Brush the eel chunks with some of the olive oil, season them with salt and pepper, then place them under a medium grill. Grill them for 3 minutes on each side and then place them in an ovenproof dish with 12 tbsp olive oil, 2 tbsp vinegar, 1 tbsp mint and two-thirds of the garlic. Bake the eel in the oven for 10 minutes.

Meanwhile, cook the green beans in salted boiling water for 3 minutes until al dente, and mix together the remaining olive oil, vinegar, mint and garlic to make a dressing.

Toss the freshly cooked green beans in the dressing and serve the eel on top.

Lamb medallions

with morels

15g dried morels
6 tbsp water
500g cleaned lamb fillet, on the rack
60g unsalted butter
1 onion, peeled and finely chopped
2 tbsp red wine
salt and freshly ground black pepper
fresh parsley, chopped, to garnish

Soak the morels in the water for 30 minutes, drain them and reserve the liquor. Preheat the oven to 220°C (gas mark 6). Season the lamb, and then fry it in an ovenproof pan for 2 minutes on each side in half of the butter. Set it aside and add the onion to the same pan, frying it gently for 3 minutes until golden brown. Add the drained morels, with a little of the reserved liquor and the wine, salt and pepper. Next add the rest of the butter, return the lamb to the pan and place it in the oven for 5 minutes. Garnish with chopped parsley, and serve hot, with either new potatoes or gratin dauphinoise.

Antonio Carluccio
The Neal Street Restaurant

Cioccolato cioccolato

400g dark bitter chocolate
1.2 litres double cream
1.2 litres milk
600ml dark rum
1.5 litres water
for the coulis
225g mixed berries
85g caster sugar
2 tbsp water
summer fruits to garnish (optional)

In a bain-marie, melt down the chocolate, adding 600ml of the cream, the milk, the rum and the water, and reduce the mixture down to a smooth liquid. Remove it from the heat, allow it to cool slightly, then add the rest of the cream. Pour the mixture into ramekin dishes and chill in the fridge for a couple of hours.

For the coulis: heat the ingredients together in a pan, and reduce them to a sauce consistency before passing the coulis through a fine sieve. Remove the dessert from the ramekins and serve with the coulis.

Martin Caws
Mirabelle

Martin Caws
Mirabelle

I had no intention of becoming a chef – it just turned out that way. Once I started my first job as a commis, it opened my eyes and I knew it was something that I wanted to pursue.

To become Head Chef of the Mirabelle has taken me ten years, working through the kitchens of chefs such as Raymond Blanc, Tom Aitkens and Marco Pierre White.

Why the Mirabelle? The chance to lead a highly skilled team in an exclusive restaurant at the heart of London's most expensive residential area is the chance of a lifetime. We are dedicated to retaining our Michelin star, and are justifiably proud of our unique style of French cuisine that brings a touch of glamour to dining out. So all I can really say is, enjoy the selection of dishes from Mirabelle.

Pigeon foie gras

with cep sauce

4 x 70g pieces of foie gras
4 pigeon breasts, skin and fat
removed
salt and white pepper
4 savoy cabbage leaves, blanched
and refreshed
caul fat for wrapping (pig's
stomach fat)
for the cep sauce
400ml warm water
100g dried ceps
1kg chicken wings
100ml arachide oil
400ml Madeira
400ml veal stock
1/2 onion, chopped
1 sprig of thyme
1/2 head of garlic bulb

Leave the foie gras to soften at room temperature for 15 minutes. Then place one piece on top of each pigeon breast and wrap them in clingfilm, moulding the foie gras to the same shape as the pigeon. Put them in the fridge to firm for about 1–2 hours.

For the cep sauce: infuse the water with the dried ceps and leave for 20 minutes, keeping the ceps in. Roast the chicken wings in arachide oil in a pan on top of the oven until golden and crispy. Deglaze the pan with the Madeira, add the veal stock and the cep water until the liquid covers the bones, add the onion, thyme and garlic and simmer for 20 minutes. Then pass the sauce once through a colander and four times through a muslin, and discard everything except the liquor.

To prepare the dish, remove the clingfilm from the pigeon breasts, season them well, and wrap each one in a cabbage leaf. Then wrap them tightly in caul fat and steam for 6 minutes. Allow them to rest for 6 minutes, then steam for a further 6 minutes until medium rare.

To serve, place one pigeon fois gras on each plate, and carefully spoon the sauce around the edge, garnishing with some mashed potato and with some white pepper sprinkled on top.

Ballotine of salmon

Makes 10–12 pieces

for the salmon

2 x 600g sides of salmon, filleted
and trimmed
cayenne pepper
salt
1 leaf of gelatine
1 bunch fresh dill, finely chopped
1 bunch flat-leaf parsley, finely
chopped
1 bunch fresh tarragon, finely
chopped
500ml milk
500ml water
ice

for the fromage blanc

10g shallots, finely chopped
200g fromage blanc (white cheese)
1/2 clove of garlic, minced
30ml lemon juice
7g salt
6 drops tabasco
30ml double cream
10g mixed fresh herbs, finely
chopped (dill, tarragon and flat-leaf
parsley)

for the garnish

150g fresh langoustines
24 chives
60ml vinaigrette
20g ocietre caviar
50g wood sorrel to garnish

For the salmon: cure the salmon with the cayenne pepper and salt for 45 minutes, rinse then pat dry. Put one side of the salmon, skin-side down, on a piece of clingfilm. Cut the gelatine into equal strips, place them along the fillet and top with the second side of salmon, skin-side up. Roll the entire salmon in the chopped herbs, wrap it tightly in clingfilm and tie both ends securely. Place it in clean muslin, tie it at equally spaced intervals with 10 pieces of string, and poach, just covered in half milk and half water for 5 minutes per kg (about 7 minutes in total), turning it over halfway through. Remove it from the heat and allow it to rest in the liquor for the same amount of time it took to cook. Add enough ice to cool it rapidly, then remove it from the liquid and refrigerate overnight.

For the fromage blanc: sweat off the shallots in a little olive oil until soft but not coloured and allow to cool. Mix the cheese with the garlic, shallots, lemon juice, salt and tabasco. Fold in the double cream a little at a time, then add the herbs.

Blanch the langoustines for 2 minutes, refresh them in boiling water, then peel and chop them.

To prepare the dish, slice the salmon into 25mm slices and put one in the centre of each plate. Surround them with 5 quenelles of fromage blanc, topped with 2 chive tips alternated with pieces of langoustine brushed with vinaigrette and dotted with caviar. Fill the spaces in between with wood sorrel, and garnish the salmon with a spoonful of caviar.

Martin Caws
Mirabelle

Grilled sea bass
with citrus fruits

for the sea bass

4 x 400–500g sea bass, or 4 sea
bass fillets

50ml olive oil

for the saffron potatoes

20g shallots

a pinch of saffron

1 tsp olive oil

12 small potatoes, peeled and cut
into a barrel shape (Charlotte
(waxy) potatoes are best)

chicken stock, enough to cover
potatoes

for the sauce

1 litre fresh orange juice

250g unsalted butter, diced and
cold

for the garnish

8 pieces of baby fennel, trimmed

12 turned saffron potatoes (cut into
barrel shapes when raw)

8 segments of pink grapefruit, pith
removed

8 segments of orange, pith
removed

8 segments of lemon, pith removed

candied zest of citrus fruit

For the sea bass: preheat the oven to 220°C (gas mark 7). Prepare the sea
bass by removing the head, tail, rib cage and guts, trimming, de-scaling
and cleaning them thoroughly. Sear them on both sides in olive oil in a hot
ovenproof non-stick pan, then transfer them to the oven. Cook for 3–4
minutes until coloured

Cook the fennel in boiling salted water until soft.

For the saffron potatoes: preheat the oven to 220°C (gas mark 7). Sweat
the shallots in a pan with the olive oil and saffron. Roll the potatoes in the
mixture and cover them with the chicken stock. Cook in the oven for 8–10
minutes.

For the sauce: heat up the orange juice in a pan and simmer until it has
reduced to a glaze. Stir in the butter and keep it warm until required.

To prepare the dish, warm the fruit under the grill for a few moments.
Place one piece of sea bass on each plate and garnish with the fennel and
saffron potatoes. Then arrange 2 pieces of each type of fruit around the
edge with the zest, pour over the sauce and serve.

Chocolate and almond parfait

for the parfait

40g caster sugar
6ml water
15g dark chocolate
1 egg, whisked
5g clear honey
20g toasted almonds, crushed
135g double cream, semi-whipped

for the cones

67g dark chocolate
red fruits (raspberries,
blackberries, strawberries)

For the parfait: boil the sugar and water together until they reach 118°C. Meanwhile, heat the chocolate in a bain-marie until melted. Pour the sugar mixture on to the whisked eggs, stir it in, then add the chocolate, honey and almonds and carefully fold in the cream. Leave the mixture until it is set.

For the cones: cut out 4 saucer-sized circles of baking parchment. Make a cut into the centre, and wrap the parchment round to create a cone-shape, securing it with sellotape. Melt the chocolate in a bain-marie, then coat the inside of each cone with a thin layer, allowing it to cool. Fill each one with the almond mixture, and transfer them to the freezer for 2–3 hours.

To serve, peel off the paper from the frozen cones, place them in the centre of the plate and garnish with red fruits.

Leigh Diggins
Sonny's

Leigh Diggins
Sonny's

I never had any great ambitions to be a chef. The cookery course I did was more by default than anything else, but when I realised the creative and artistic scope involved in cooking, I was hooked. I trained for two years in Switzerland, before training under the three-star consultant chef Michel Lorain. Then, after four years working as Senior Sous Chef at the Michelin-starred Capital Hotel, Knightsbridge, I became Head Chef at the Hoste Arms Hotel, Burnham Market in Norfolk.

For me, the confines of Michelin-starred restaurants are too strict, though. I want to deliver fine food in a more relaxed environment and Sonny's is ideal for this – the perfect neighbourhood restaurant nestling in flourishing, leafy Barnes. It first opened in April 1986 and I joined in 1997 as Head Chef, creating modern British food amid the clean lines of its modern interior. The formula has been so successful that some of our regulars visit us three or four times a week – be that for a major celebration or just a quick and simple supper.

Whatever you fancy, the quality of our food and the care we take over serving you never wavers. It's this consistency that keeps Sonny's full, and this is the reason my long-term ambition is to open my own restaurant based on the fun I have here.

Cornish crab

with artichoke, ginger, tomato, samphire and dandelion leaf salad

200g Cornish crab meat (white only), picked
1 tsp mayonnaise (home-made or bought)
juice of 1 lime
pinch of salt
pinch of cayenne pepper
10g chives, chopped
4 globe artichokes
dash of lemon juice
4 plum tomatoes, diced
20g ginger, finely chopped
100g samphire
tomato oil, ready-made
aged balsamic vinegar
1 head of white dandelion leaves, picked

Pick over the crab meat to remove any unwanted shell and bind it with the mayonnaise, lime juice, salt, cayenne and chives. Cut off the outside leaves of the artichokes and hollow the middles. Cook them in boiling salted water with a dash of lemon juice for a few minutes. When cooked, drain them off, allow them to cool and slice each into 3 discs, dicing the trimmings.

To prepare the dish, combine the diced artichoke trimmings, ginger, tomato and samphire, assemble them in the middle of a plate and dress them with tomato oil and aged balsamic vinegar. Layer up 3 artichoke discs with the crab mayonnaise in between, and place the picked dandelion leaves on top of the salad to garnish.

Leigh Diggins
Sonny's

Pan-fried scallops

with a pea pancake, girolles, pea and mint purée and a
tomato and lemon dressing

for the pea and mint purée
25g unsalted butter
1 shallot, finely chopped
1 clove of garlic, finely chopped
250g frozen peas
4 fresh mint leaves
100 ml dry white wine
400 ml water

for the pancake mix
225g frozen peas
1 whole egg
1 egg yoke
120g plain flour
6 fresh mint leaves
120 double cream
salt and black pepper
1 tbsp olive oil

for the dressing
juice of 1 lemon
1 tbsp olive oil
sea salt and black pepper

other ingredients
16 large scallops
1 tbsp olive oil
500g spinach
4 plum tomatoes, blanched,
skinned and deseeded
100g fresh peas
100g girolle mushrooms
unsalted butter
8 chive tips, to garnish
4 sprigs chervil, to garnish

For the pea and mint purée: melt the butter in a frying pan, add the shallot
and garlic, and sweat them off until soft. Add the frozen peas, mint leaves,
wine and water and cook until soft. Blitz, pass the purée through a sieve,
and set on one side until needed.

For the pancake mix: place the peas, egg, flour and mint in a food
processor and blitz into a purée. Add the cream and season to taste. Heat
a little olive oil in a frying pan, and spoon in enough of the mix to make a
pancake that is 8 cm across. Cook for about 30–40 seconds on each side
until golden brown and keep these warm until needed.

For the dressing: combine the lemon juice and olive oil, then season with
sea salt and pepper.

To prepare the dish, put the scallops in a frying pan and colour them on
both sides for 20 seconds in a little olive oil. Cook the spinach in salted
boiling water for 10 seconds, then drain. Warm through the diced tomato,
cook the fresh peas in boiling salted water for about 6 minutes, and sauté
the girolles in a little butter for 30 seconds.

To serve, combine the spinach, tomatoes, peas and girolles, and place
them in the centre of the plate. Put a pancake on top, then the scallops,
then a spoonful of purée, and garnish with 2 chive tips and a sprig of
chervil.

Grilled fillet of veal

with a tartlet of deep-fried sweetbreads, liquorice glace
and white onion sauce

4 x 200 veal fillet steaks
500g spinach
250g short-crust pastry
12 baby carrots

for the white onion sauce
25g unsalted butter
1 Spanish white onion, peeled and
chopped
1 clove of garlic, crushed
1 sprig of thyme
350ml dry white wine
350ml chicken stock
350ml double cream
salt
pinch of cayenne pepper

for the liquorice glace
75ml liquorice compound
300ml red wine jus (or a bought
good quality red wine sauce)

for the veal sweetbreads
500g veal heart sweetbreads
1 carrot, cut in half
1 leek, cut in half
1 stick of celery, chopped
1 onion, chopped
sprig fresh thyme
1 fresh bay leaf
10 black peppercorns
1 litre duck fat
3 shallots, roughly chopped
3 cloves of garlic, roughly cut
sea salt

for the button onions
12 button onions
25g unsalted butter
25g caster sugar
salt and black pepper

For the white onion sauce: melt the butter in a pan, then add the onion, garlic and thyme and cook slowly them until the onion is soft but not coloured. Add the wine and stock, bring it to the boil and reduce by half. Add the cream, bring it to the boil again and simmer for 5 minutes, seasoning with salt and a pinch of cayenne. Pour the sauce into a liquidiser, blend, then pass it through a sieve. Leave it on one side until needed.

For the liquorice glace: put the liquorice compound (which can be bought from a specialist store) and jus in a pan and reduce the mixture by two-thirds.

For the veal sweetbreads: rinse the sweetbreads in cold water for 30 minutes, then put them into a pan with the carrot, leek, celery, onion, thyme, bay leaf and peppercorns. Cover with cold water, bring everything to the boil, then simmer for 1 hour. Allow the sweetbreads to cool in the liquor, then remove them and peel off the skin, sinew and any fatty bits. Break them into walnut-sized pieces. Discard the cooking liquor. Then place the duck fat, shallots, garlic, remaining thyme and sea salt in a pan and heat until the fat melts. Add the veal sweetbreads, cook very slowly for 1 hour, then allow them to cool and remove them from the fat.

For the tartlet: preheat the oven to 180°C (gas mark 4). Roll out the pastry to 2mm thick. Line a pastry tartlet dish with it and press it down with an empty tartlet dish on top. Rest it for a couple of hours then put it in the oven for 8 minutes with the empty dish still on top.

For the button onions: cover the onions in a frying pan with the butter, sugar, a little water and a pinch of salt and cracked black pepper, and cook them on a high heat until all of the water evaporates and the onions are caramelised.

For the carrots: prepare the baby carrots and boil them in salted water for a few minutes until tender.

To prepare the dish, place the sweetbreads in a deep-fat fryer and cook them for about 2 minutes until golden brown. Grill the veal steaks on each side for 1 minute. Sauté the spinach in a little butter and a pinch of salt and pepper, then cook it down until soft, drain it, then place it in the middle of a plate. Put the steak on top, with the tartlet over this, and fill it with the sweetbreads and glazed button onions. Pour liquorice glace over the sweetbreads, and place the baby carrots over the sweetbreads. To finish, warm the white onion sauce and pour it around the plate.

Raspberry-flavoured desserts

for the raspberry purée
600g raspberries
100g caster sugar

for the jelly
150ml Muscat wine
150ml stock syrup
2 leaves of gelatine
24 raspberries

for the parfait
225g caster sugar
225g water
8 egg yolks
500ml raspberry purée
1 litre double cream, 3/4 whipped

for the Alaska
4 scoops of vanilla ice-cream
4 almond biscuit discs, bought or home-made
4 sable biscuit discs, bought or home-made
12 raspberries
150g caster sugar
150ml water
3 egg whites

to garnish
100g raspberry purée
100g clotted cream,

For the raspberry purée: cook the raspberries in the sugar until soft. Put them in the liquidiser, blitz them until puréed, then pass it through a chinois and put to one side until needed.

For the jelly: this can be made the day before. Heat the Muscat and stock syrup until simmering. Soak the gelatine in cold water until soft, remove it and squeeze out any excess water. Add this to the Muscat mix, and allow it to cool. Meanwhile, take four 50g moulds and, when the mixture is cool, pour in just enough to line the bottom. Put them in the fridge for 1 hour until set. When ready, add 6 raspberries to each, and pour in the remaining jelly mixture to cover them. Leave them in the fridge to set for a few hours.

For the parfait: place the sugar in a thick-bottomed pan and cover with the water. Bring it to the soft-ball stage for 5 minutes. Place the egg yolks into a blender at full speed until white, then gradually add the soft-balled sugar and mix until it is stiff. Add the raspberry purée (making sure that you reserve 100g for the garnish), fold in the three-quarters whipped cream, spoon it into the moulds and freeze them overnight.

For the Alaska: preheat the oven to 200°C (gas mark 6). Place a ball of vanilla ice-cream on an almond biscuit disc and top it with a sable biscuit disc. Position 3 raspberries around the ice-cream. Boil the water and the caster sugar to the soft-ball stage, then place them in a blender. Add the egg whites and the soft-ball sugar and blend for 10 minutes until the mixture is stiff and white. Pipe the meringue mix over the berries and ice-cream, and place them in the oven for 5 minutes until the meringue is crisp on the outside and slightly golden.

To serve, spoon a ring of raspberry coulis on a cold plate. Place the Alaska at one point. Turn out the jelly and place it at another, with a little clotted cream on the top, and position the parfait at the side.

William Drabble
Aubergine

William Drabble
Aubergine

Cooking is something that I have always wanted to do. After working as chef de partie and sous chef in a number of London's top establishments – places like The Capital, Nico Ninety Park Lane and Pied à Terre – I headed North to Grasmere in 1997 where Michael's Nook beckoned. This is a classic country house hotel and was the place where I gained my first Michelin star – the first one the restaurant had ever been awarded as well.

A year later and I was back in London again, this time to take over after Gordon Ramsey at Chelsea's Aubergine where I am the chef/patron. It was like starting from scratch in many ways, but my reputation for producing quality modern French cuisine stood me in good stead. On only the second evening, with a totally new team in both the kitchens and dining room, someone arrived from Michelin. And against all the odds I retained my star.

The consistency of my food, combined with service that is warm and attentive without ever being overbearing, has helped to ensure that the restaurant has gone from strength to strength. We use only the freshest of ingredients: scallops and lobster from Scotland; lamb from Cumbria; chicken and duck from Lancashire; truffles from France and Italy; fois gras from France; and seasonal fruit and vegetables – produce that ensures the best possible flavour in every dish.

The recipes that follow are my favourites – dishes that sum up the Aubergine style of cooking. Yes, a couple may seem complicated compared with your average recipe book and yes, you will have to begin preparing various elements well in advance if you wish to experience them at their best. But then again, Aubergine is not your average restaurant, and in the end it is the care and preparation that go into the cooking process that make the difference between food, and food to remember.

Assiette of duck

for the duck

1 whole duck (including livers, gizzards, neck and head)

for the strong chicken stock

3kg chicken necks

1kg chicken wing

water, to cover necks and wings

3 onions, chopped

4 carrots, chopped

5 sticks of celery, chopped

1 leek, chopped

3 cloves of garlic, halved

6 sprigs of thyme

for the duck leg confit

1.75 litres duck fat

1 onion, roughly chopped

1 carrot, roughly chopped

2 sticks of celery, roughly chopped

3 cloves of garlic, halved

salt

1 tsp peppercorns

duck legs (from whole duck)

duck gizzards (from whole duck)

for the stuffed neck

2 tbsp duck fat

1 shallot, finely chopped

2 tbsp port

2 tbsp brandy

2 tbsp Madeira

2 sprigs of thyme

duck liver, trimmed

100g foie gras, diced

salt and white pepper

duck neck skin flap, cleaned and still in a cylindrical shape

reserved duck fat from the duck leg confit

knob of unsalted butter

For the duck: remove the head with a large knife, then go to the bottom of the neck and cut the skin all the way around, pulling off the neck flap so that it is inside out. Remove any excess fat, blood and unwanted tubes and so forth, turn it back the right way around and place it in the fridge. This will be used like a sausage skin. Chop off the neck and cut it into pieces. Remove the duck's wings and chop these up too, and cut off the legs, reserving these for the duck confit. Remove and trim the breasts, refrigerating them until needed, and trim the livers and gizzards, reserving the trimmed gizzards for the confit. Chop up the carcass, reserving the bones for the sauce.

For the strong chicken stock: put the chicken necks and wings in a large pan and cover them with plenty of water. Bring this to the boil, skim the surface and add the vegetables. Cook slowly for 4 hours, skimming regularly, then pass the stock through a fine chinois, then 4 layers of muslin, before pouring it back in the pan and reducing the stock until you have about 1 litre – to be used in both the duck sauce and turnips.

For the duck leg confit: bring the vegetables and peppercorns up to the boil in the duck fat, and season them to taste with salt. Add the duck legs and gizzards, and bring the temperature back up again, before cooking them very slowly until the meat falls off the bone. Do not allow the mixture to boil. When cooked, let the mixture cool and remove the duck meat and gizzards from the fat. Pour the remaining mixture through a fine sieve, reserving the duck fat and discarding the vegetables. Then break up the meat so that there is no skin, bone or veins, cut the gizzards into 3 pieces, and put them in a bowl.

For the stuffed neck: put 2 tbsp duck fat into a pan and sweat off the shallot so that it is soft but not coloured. Add the alcohol and thyme, and slowly reduce the mixture until it has a syrupy consistency. Pass it through a chinois on to the broken up duck confit. Purée the livers in a blender and add them to the duck confit along with the fois gras, mixing them together and seasoning them with salt and pepper. Then take the duck neck skin and tie a knot in the narrower end. Fill the skin up with the duck confit mixture, tie a knot in the other end and place it in the fridge until needed. Then take the reserved duck fat from the confit, and poach (not boil) the neck for 30 minutes on a low heat, before allowing it to cool, removing it from the fat and refrigerating it well. When thoroughly chilled, untie the knots, remove the meat from the skin and cut the sausage into 4 pieces, keeping it cool until needed.

for the duck sauce

100ml vegetable oil

100g unsalted butter

bones from duck, chopped

2 shallots, peeled and sliced

3 cloves of garlic, halved

60g button mushrooms

200ml Madeira

600ml strong chicken stock

3 sprigs of thyme

for the lyonnaise onions

4 large onions

50g unsalted butter

1 clove of garlic, crushed

3 sprigs of thyme, washed and picked

salt and white pepper

for the lyonnaise potatoes

2 large potatoes, peeled and sliced (4 mm)

275ml duck fat

15g unsalted butter

salt and white pepper

For the duck sauce: heat up a pan and add the oil and butter. When these start to foam, add the duck bones and cook them until golden brown. Add the shallots and garlic, and cook these until soft before adding the mushrooms and cooking them until tender. Drain off the fat and deglaze the pan with the Madeira, before putting the bones back in again with the stock and bringing the mixture to the boil. Skim the surface and add the thyme, cooking slowly for 40 minutes. If the sauce reduces too much, add a little extra water. When ready, pass the sauce through a fine chinois, then through a muslin cloth, and set it on one side. Once settled, remove any fat from the surface, put it back in a pan and reduce it to a thin syrup. Adjust the seasoning to taste and keep on one side until needed.

For the duck breast: heat up a non-stick pan until it is hot. Score the breasts at 5mm intervals to create a criss-cross pattern, and season them with salt and pepper. Then place the breasts skin-side down in the pan, and cook them slowly until the skin becomes crisp. When blood spots begin to appear on the top of the breasts, turn them over and cook them for another 30–45 seconds. Remove them from the pan and allow them to rest skin-side down in a warm place for 5–10 minutes.

For the lyonnaise onions: peel and cut the onions through their root. Remove the roots and cut them into 3 mm slices. Melt the butter in a pan, and add the onion, garlic and thyme leaves, together with a little salt and pepper. Cook the mixture slowly until well caramelised, then drain of any excess butter.

for the turnips

12 baby turnips

30g unsalted

100ml Madeira

salt

300ml strong chicken stock

for the cabbage confit

1 small savoy cabbage

3 slices of streaky bacon, cut into lardons

1 tbsp duck fat

100ml double cream

salt and white pepper

for the fois gras

4 slices of fois gras, 1 cm thick

salt and white pepper

For the lyonnaise potatoes: cut the potato slices into 4–5 mm discs with a cutter, allowing 3 per portion (12 discs in all). Then poach the discs in the duck fat until just cooked, before removing them from the fat and allowing them to cool.

For the turnips: blanch the turnips in boiling salted water for 1 minute, then refresh them in iced water. Scrape off the skins and dry them. Heat up the butter in a pan and, when it starts to foam, add the turnips and allow them to caramelise slowly. Drain off the butter, add the Madeira and reduce it until it is thick and syrupy. Then season it and add the stock. Bring everything to the boil, place a piece of butter paper on the top and cook slowly until the turnips are tender. Once cooked, reduce the cooking liquor quickly until the turnips are glazed.

For the cabbage confit: discard the dark-green outer leaves from the cabbage, and remove the remaining leaves one by one, reserving all the green ones and discarding the yellow heart. Then remove the centre stalk from each cabbage leaf, wash and chiffonade them finely, and blanch them in boiling salted water until soft. Refresh the cabbage in ice-cold water for a few minutes, drain it, squeeze it out and place it on absorbant paper. Fry the bacon lardons in the duck fat until they start to curl up, and mix in the cabbage and cream, cooking them slowly until the mixture starts to thicken. Season with salt and pepper and set on one side until needed.

For the fois gras: place the fois gras slices in a red-hot pan, allow them to colour, then turn them over and cook them slowly until they are warmed through. Drain them and serve immediately.

To prepare the dish, reheat the duck neck and onions in separate pans in a little butter. Sauté the potatoes in a little extra duck fat and butter until golden brown, then season with salt and pepper and drain. Warm the sauce through, reheat the turnips in a couple of tablespoons of water, and slice up the warm duck breasts. Arrange the cabbage on the plate with the sliced duck breast on top. Then place the turnips on the plate with the duck neck on top, and then the potatoes with the onions and sautéd fois gras on top, pouring the sauce around.

Fillet of sea bass

with roasted artichokes, tomato confit, fennel, sweet
pepper purée and basil oil

for the pepper purée
200ml olive oil
5 red peppers, finely chopped
salt

for the basil oil
1 bunch of fresh basil
200ml vegetable oil
salt

for the tomato confit
8 tomatoes, skinned, quartered
and deseeded
2 cloves of garlic, cut into paper-
thin slices
8 sprigs of thyme, cut into 4
pieces each
3 tbsp olive oil
salt
1 tsp icing sugar

for the baby artichokes
12 baby artichokes
400ml olive oil
150ml dry white wine
2 shallots, sliced
1 clove of garlic, crushed
1 sprig of thyme
salt and white pepper
8 fresh basil leaves, chopped

for the braised fennel
1 shallot, sliced
1 clove of garlic, crushed
1 sprig of thyme
1/2 star anise
200ml olive oil
4 fennel bulbs, trimmed and halved
pinch of salt

For the pepper purée: heat up the olive oil in a pan, add the peppers and season them with salt. Cook them slowly for 10–15 minutes until soft, blitz them into a purée, and pass this through a chinois. Keep the purée on one side until needed.

For the basil oil: blanch the basil in boiling salted water for 3 minutes, then drain it off and squeeze out any excess water. Place it in a liquidiser and blitz it with the oil for 3 minutes, before returning it to a pan and bringing it up to the boil, stirring continuously until the oil splits out of the purée. Then hang the mixture up in a damp muslin cloth and allow the oil to drip through. Reserve the oil and discard the remaining purée.

For the tomato confit: preheat the oven to 150°C (gas mark 2) and line a baking tray with aluminium foil. Place the tomato petals on to the tray, and lay a slice of garlic on top of each, followed by a piece of thyme. Pour the olive oil over the top, and season lightly with the salt and icing sugar. Then place the tray in the oven and leave the tomatoes until they have half dried out.

For the baby artichokes: remove the outer leaves from the artichokes until they are yellow and tender, peel the stalks down with a peeler until all the green stringy skin is removed, and trim the tops off to halfway down. Then trim the stalks until they are 1¹/₂–2 cm in length. Warm up a little of the olive oil in a lidded pan and sweat off the shallots, garlic and thyme until soft but not coloured. Add the prepared artichokes, wine and remaining olive oil, season to taste, cover with the lid and boil vigorously until the wine has reduced and the artichokes are cooked. If the wine reduces before the artichokes are ready, add a little water and continue cooking. Leave the pan to cool, then slice the artichokes into 3–4 pieces. Put them back into the cooking liquor and keep them on one side until needed.

For the braised fennel: sweat off the shallots, garlic, thyme and star anise in the olive oil, then add the fennel, salt and enough water to cover everything and bring the mixture to the boil. Reduce the heat, cover the pan with a piece of silicon paper and cook the fennel gently until it is soft (do not let it boil). Then remove the fennel from the cooking liquor, allow it to cool, and cut it into 6mm slices.

For the sea bass: preheat the oven to 240°C (gas mark 9). Wash the fish in cold water, and remove any remaining scales and bones. Dry the fillets, and cut each into 2, trimming the edges to neaten them up. Then score the skin at 5mm intervals with a sharp knife. Heat up an ovenproof pan

for the sea bass

1 x 1.35–8kg sea bass, scaled,
gutted, filleted and pin-boned
juice of ¹/₂ a lemon
salt
2 tbsp olive oil

until hot, add the olive oil and place the fillets skin side down, frying them for 1 minute to allow the skin to begin crisping up. Then put them in the red-hot oven for 3–4 minutes until cooked, remove them, turn them skin-side up, and season them with salt and lemon, before draining off any cooking liquor.

To prepare the dish, lightly warm the purée through in a pan. Reheat the fennel by colouring it slowly in a little olive oil and butter, and season it with salt and pepper. Likewise, reheat the artichokes by sautéing them quickly in a little olive oil, and season them with salt, pepper and a little basil, adding the tomatoes at the last minute to warm them through. Place the pepper purée on a plate, with the fennel on top. Then place the artichokes and tomatoes on top of this, with the sea bass to finish. Drizzle the basil oil around the edge and serve.

Warm salad of roasted vegetables

16 spears of asparagus

for the artichokes

2 large artichokes

400ml olive oil

150ml dry white wine

2 shallots, sliced

1 clove of garlic, crushed

1 sprig of thyme

salt and white pepper

8 fresh basil leaves, chopped

for the asparagus purée

125g unsalted butter

250g asparagus, chopped up small

salt and white pepper

for the truffle dressing

3 large shallots, finely diced

150ml olive oil

4 sprigs of thyme, picked

salt and white pepper

25g truffle, chopped

for the curly endive

1 curly endive

salt

balsamic vinegar

for the rocket

125g rocket

2 drops of balsamic vinegar

for the morels

12 large morels, trimmed, halved, washed and drained on a cloth

1 tbsp unsalted butter

salt

other ingredients

olive oil

unsalted butter

For the truffle dressing: sweat off the shallots in the olive oil and thyme, season them with salt and pepper and, when soft, allow them to cool. Add the chopped truffle, cover and refrigerate for 3–4 days.

For the asparagus: remove the tough ends of the asparagus, blanch them in boiling salted water until tender, and refresh them in iced water, leaving them on one side until needed.

For the artichokes: remove the outer leaves from the artichokes, snap off the stalk and cut the top off just above the heart. Peel the heart with a peeler until it is rounded and white, then remove the spines from the centre with a spoon. Warm up a little of the olive oil in a lidded pan and sweat off the shallots, garlic and thyme until soft but not coloured. Add the prepared artichokes, wine and remaining olive oil, season to taste, cover with the lid and boil vigorously until the wine has reduced and the artichokes are cooked. If the wine reduces before the artichokes are ready, add a little water and continue cooking. Leave the pan to cool, then slice the artichokes into 3–4 pieces. Keep them on one side in the cooking liquor until needed.

For the asparagus purée: melt the butter in a pan and add the asparagus and seasoning. Cook it quickly in the foaming butter until it is just tender, blitz it into a purée, pass it through a chinois and reserve.

For the curly endive: pick the yellow leaves from the heart of the endive, wash them and drain them well. Then place the endive in a bowl, and season it at the last minute with a little salt, some truffle oil and a couple of drops of balsamic vinegar.

For the rocket: pick through the leaves to remove the stalks, and dress them with a little truffle dressing and a couple of drops of balsamic.

To prepare the dish, roast the asparagus and artichokes in a little butter and oil in a pan until golden, then drain them off. Gently warm through the asparagus purée in a small pan, and gently cook the morels for 2–3 minutes in the butter and salt until soft. Then place the rocket leaves neatly on a plate, with the artichokes, morels and asparagus stacked neatly on top. Spoon over the asparagus purée, and place a ball of curly endive on top to finish.

Assiette of cherries

for the almond ice-cream
75g flaked almonds
250ml milk
3 egg yolks
50g caster sugar
125ml double cream

for the beignet soufflé
125ml water
60g unsalted butter
pinch of salt
pinch of caster sugar
60g plain flour
2–3 eggs, beaten
vegetable oil for deep-frying
vanilla sugar (caster sugar
infused with a vanilla pod for
2 days)

for the kirsch jelly
250ml water
100g caster sugar
20 cherries, destoned
35ml kirsch
3 leaves of gelatine

for the sauce mousseline
2 egg yolks
seeds from 1 vanilla pod
55ml water
50g caster sugar
55ml double cream, lightly
whipped

for the cherry compote
200ml black cherry purée (ready-
made)
2 tbsp icing sugar
20 cherries, destoned
1 tsp cornflour
2 tsp water
a dash of cherry brandy

For the almond ice-cream: preheat the oven to 150°C (gas mark 2) and roast the almonds slowly on a baking tray until golden brown. Put them into a pan, add the milk, and bring this to the boil. Leave it to cool so that the almond flakes can infuse into the milk. Whisk together the egg yolks and sugar until light and fluffy, bring the almond milk back up to the boil, and pour this over the sugar mixture a little at a time. Put it back into the pan and cook slowly until the mixture starts to thicken. Do not allow it to boil. Add the cream, pass it through a fine chinois and allow it to cool. Churn the mixture and allow it to freeze. Alternatively, whisk it in a metal bowl and place it in the freezer overnight – whisking it regularly throughout.

For the beignet soufflé: place the water, butter, salt and sugar in a pan and bring them up to a simmer. Add the flour, and cook the mixture until it is a smooth paste and leaves the side of the pan. Put the paste into a mixer and beat it for 2–3 minutes, gradually adding the eggs until the paste reaches a smooth piping consistency. Then place it into a piping bag, pipe walnut-sized amounts on to silicon paper, and deep-fry them in the vegetable oil for 3–4 minutes until golden brown. Drain off any excess oil, roll them in the vanilla sugar, and cut them almost in half. While still hot, place a quenelle of ice-cream in the centre of each and put them in the freezer until required.

For the kirsch jelly: bring the water and sugar to the boil, then add the cherries and poach them for a couple of minutes until cooked. Add the kirsch, and leave the cherries to marinate on one side for 3–4 hours. Remove the cherries, and warm up 285ml of the syrup they were marinating in. Dissolve the gelatine in this and then add the remaining syrup. Place the cherries into small dariole moulds, cover them with the jelly and place them in the fridge until set.

For the sauce mousseline: whisk the egg yolks with the vanilla seeds until light and aerated. Meanwhile, boil the sugar and water together until they reach the soft ball stage, and pour this on to the egg yolks. Continue to whisk until the mixture is cold, fold in the cream and chill until needed.

For the cherry compote: bring the cherry purée to the boil, add the icing sugar and cherries, and cook them slowly for 2–3 minutes until softened. Dissolve the cornflour in the water, add this to the cherry sauce and bring the mixture back up to the boil until it has thickened. Allow the sauce to cool slightly, let it back with a little cherry brandy, and set it on one side until needed.

for the cherry yoghurt mousse
1 1/2 leaves of gelatine
125g black cherry purée (ready-made)
110ml natural yoghurt
75ml double cream
50g caster sugar
2 egg whites
other ingredients
100g dark chocolate
12 cherries to garnish

For the cherry yoghurt mousse: soften the gelatine in a little water, squeeze out any excess moisture, and add this to the cherry purée, folding in the yoghurt and cream when it begins to set. Put the sugar and some water into a pan, and boil them to the soft ball stage. Meanwhile, whisk the egg whites until they start to peak, then pour on the boiling syrup and continue to whisk until the mixture is cold and you have a thick meringue. Fold this into the cherry cream mousse and put it in the fridge to set – using this the same day.

For the chocolate cylinders: cut a piece of silicon paper into 5cm strips and roll these into tubes, securing them with tape. Melt the chocolate in a bain-marie, then smooth it thinly around the rolled paper. Leave the cylinders to set in the fridge, removing the paper when ready to serve.

To prepare the dish, pipe the cherry and yoghurt mousse into the chocolate cylinders and top each with a cherry. Place a spoonful of the mousseline sauce on to the plate and turn out the kirsch jelly on top. Warm the cherry compote through and add this to the plate, serving with a cut beignet on top and almond ice-cream in the middle.

Chris Galvin
Orrery

Chris Galvin
Orrery

I began cooking at the age of fifteen after knocking on Anthony Worrell Thompson's door and getting a job with him. Twenty-seven years later I have been lucky enough to have spent time in some of the best restaurants in France. This is largely because every year I spend one week of my holiday over there on a *stage*, or placement, looking at new and different techniques and absorbing the atmosphere to give me new ideas and inspiration.

French cuisine is my first – and only – love. It is what I know and understand, so it will come as no surprise that Orrery is a French restaurant. Here we allow the ingredients to take centre stage by selecting the best and, as you will see on the pages that follow, treating them simply to show them off to their best advantage.

I opened the restaurant in October 1997 with my brother Jeff, a phenomenal chef who I admire greatly – even though we are related! In fact, I think I'm right in saying that we are the only British brothers ever to have been awarded separate Michelin stars for our work. But I must also pay tribute to my friend and mentor, Paul Gayler, now at the Lanesborough. Working with him at Inigo Jones was the experience of a lifetime and in a sense I owe him everything.

My favourite food is actually very straightforward – a roasted shoulder of lamb and green salad, with an apple tart fin to finish. The recipes I have chosen for this book all reflect the Orrery's philosophy – good ingredients treated simply. I hope you enjoy them.

Ballotine of foie gras

with poached pear and balsamic gelée

for the gelée
250ml stock syrup
100ml balsamic vinegar (8-year-old)
1 leaf of gelatine

for the pear
1 pear, peeled
stock syrup to cover

for the foie gras
700g foie gras
750ml bottle Sauternes wine
15g caster sugar
25g salt

other ingredients
olive oil to taste
Fleur de Sel to taste

For the gelée: pour the stock syrup and the balsamic vinegar into a pan, bring them to the boil and skim. Soak the gelatine leaf in water for 5 minutes, then take it out and drain. Add this to the balsamic mixture and pour on to a small tray. Place this in the fridge to set.

For the pear: cover the pear in stock syrup and bring it to the boil, simmering until cooked. Remove it from the heat and leave it to cool.

For the foie gras: leave the foie gras at room temperature for 2 hours, then make an incision down the middle and pull out the middle vein. Dissolve the wine, sugar and salt, put the foie gras in the marinade and leave it for 2 hours. Drain and then roll the foie gras tightly in clingfilm, tying it at each end. At the restaurant we boil a large bain-marie and gently poach the foie gras until it reaches 42°C in the middle. Ice is then placed in the water to cool it, after which you can transfer the foie gras to the fridge.

To prepare the dish, cut the pear into 1cm cubes and place 5 around each plate. With a hot knife cut the gelée into triangles and place them in between each piece of pear. Slice the foie gras with a hot knife, place it in the centre of each plate, season it with olive oil and Fleur de Sel and serve – perhaps as we do at Orrery with Pain Poîlane bread.

8 red mullet (fillets to be 75–100g)

for the bouillabaisse

50ml olive oil

100g mirepoix (fennel, celery, carrot, onion, garlic, leeks)

red mullet bones, from fillets

1 clove of garlic, crushed

1 star anise

2 coriander seeds

2 white peppercorns

25ml dry white wine

5ml Noilly Prat

200ml tomato juice

350g potato, thinly sliced

dash of Pernod

1 pinch of saffron

1 tbsp whipping cream

salt and black pepper

for the saffron mash

1 large potato, chopped

1 pinch of saffron

for the rouille

1 raw egg yolk

1 cooked egg yolk

1 large clove of garlic

1/2 red chilli, deseeded

50ml olive oil, fruity (le blanc)

salt, pepper and lemon juice

for the brandade

100g salt cod, soaked for 24 hours

100ml milk

1 clove of garlic, crushed

50ml olive oil

1 large potato

1 pinch of saffron

black pepper

lemon juice to taste

other ingredients

200g washed spinach

15g unsalted butter

1 tbsp olive oil

12 large diver scallops, cleaned

sea salt

lemon juice

12 baby leeks, cooked

picked herbs (chive, chervil, dill)

Seared scallops and red mullet

with a sauce bouillabaisse

For the bouillabaisse: marinate the bones, garlic, star anise, coriander seeds and white peppercorns in 25ml of the olive oil for 24 hours. Caramelise the vegetables in the remaining olive oil in a thick-bottomed pan, add the bones and marinade and roast off for 10 minutes on top of the stove. Deglaze with the wine and Noilly Prat, reduce to a glaze and add the tomato juice, potato and a little water. Cook for 45 minutes on a low heat, blend in a food processor and pass through a fine sieve. Finish with a splash of Pernod, the saffron and a little cream, salt and pepper.

For the saffron mash: cover the potato with salted water, bring it to the boil, skim the surface and add the saffron. Cook until soft and then purée to a smooth mash. Set aside until required in both the rouille and brandade.

For the rouille: put the raw egg yolk, garlic, chilli and 2 tbsp saffron mash in the blender, and slowly drizzle in the olive oil as if making mayonnaise. Finish with seasoning and a little lemon juice.

For the salt cod brandade: wash the soaked salt cod, then heat the milk with the garlic and lightly poach the fish for 10 minutes. When cooked take the cod out and set it aside to cool. In another pan warm the olive oil, flake in the fish and mix it to a smooth paste. Add the remaining saffron mash, check the taste and correct the seasoning with pepper and lemon juice. Do not add salt as the salt in the cod will be sufficient.

To prepare the dish, sauté the spinach in the butter for 1 minute until just cooked and set it aside. In a non-stick pan with a little olive oil gently fry the scallops and red mullet fillets for 2 minutes on one side, then 1 minute on the other side, being careful not to overcook them. Remove them from the pan and sprinkle them with sea salt and lemon.

Warm 4 plates and drop 3 tablespoonfuls of brandade along the middle of each, leaving space to put 2 tablespoonfuls of spinach in between. Place 1 scallop on each brandade and 1 red mullet fillet on each pile of spinach. Flick the rouille down on each side of the plate (at the restaurant we use a squeezy bottle), and place 1 cooked baby leek on each scallop. Warm up the bouillabaisse sauce, buzz it with a hand blender to a foam, spoon it over each mullet fillet and finish with a pluche of fresh picked herbs.

Fillet of beef

with girolles, baby leeks and a foie gras bonbon

for the Madeira jus

1 tbsp vegetable oil

3 shallots, peeled and finely chopped

40g mushrooms, sliced and finely chopped

2 cloves of garlic, peeled and chopped

1 sprig of thyme

1/2 bay leaf

300ml Madeira

300ml veal stock

100ml chicken stock

salt and pepper

for the foie gras bonbon

120g foie gras, 1st grade

1 large potato, Maris Piper or Cyprus

seasoned flour

100ml clarified unsalted butter

other ingredients

4 x 180g fillets of beef

salt and freshly milled black pepper

50g clarified unsalted butter

12 baby leeks

200g girolle mushrooms, cleaned

200g spinach, washed

2 shallots, peeled and finely chopped

For the Madeira jus: heat the vegetable oil in a large pan and sauté the shallots, mushrooms, garlic, thyme and bay leaf until golden. Deglaze with the Madeira and reduce by half. Add the stocks and bring to the boil, skimming the surface frequently. Reduce slowly until the sauce coats the back of a spoon, taste and season accordingly. At the restaurant we pass the sauce through a muslin cloth 2–3 times to produce a clear jus.

For the foie gras bonbon: take the foie gras and portion into 4. Allow it to soften, roll it into balls between your hands and put it into the fridge to harden. Cut the potato into long strands (at the restaurant we use a Chinese mandolin). Take the foie gras, roll it in some seasoned flour and slowly thread the potato strands around the sides until it is completely covered. Dip them into the clarified butter, then leave in the fridge to set. To prepare the dish, preheat the deep-fat fryer to about 175°C, and heat up a heavy black pan or non-stick frying pan. Heavily season each beef fillet with salt and pepper and gently fry them in a little clarified butter until well coloured all over and cooked to your liking – for medium–rare, about 3–4 minutes on each side. Set aside in a warm place. Bring a small pan of salted water to the boil. Drop in the leeks and cook for 1–2 minutes. Heat up a small frying pan and sauté the girolle mushrooms for 2–3 minutes in a little clarified butter until just cooked, and sauté the spinach and shallots in butter for 1 minute. Drop the 4 bonbons into the preheated fryer for 2 minutes until golden brown.

To serve, place a pile of spinach on the middle of each plate, with a small pile of leeks and girolles to one side and the bonbon to the other. Place a beef fillet on top of the spinach and pour the warm Madeira jus around the edge.

Trio de café

tiramisu, coffee semi-fredo and mocha sorbet

for the tiramisu

1 egg

70g caster sugar

1 vanilla pod, split lengthways and seeds scraped out

125g mascarpone cheese

125ml double cream

few drops Marsala

10 cullière or boudoir biscuits

150ml espresso coffee, sweetened with 20g granulated sugar

for the semi-fredo

3 egg yolks

1 tsp coffee extract

100g caster sugar

125ml double cream

2 egg whites

150ml pasteurised milk

for the mocha sorbet

500ml strong espresso coffee

500ml stock syrup

150g bitter chocolate

1 shot of Kahlua

cocoa powder for dusting

4 slices of lemon to garnish

For the tiramisu: whisk the egg, sugar and vanilla over a bain-marie until thick and pale, and allow to cool. Whisk the mascarpone and cream together, fold into the sabayon and add the Marsala. Soak the cullière biscuits in the sweetened espresso coffee, and layer these with the creamy mixture in 4 espresso cups. Allow these to set for 2–3 hours.

For the semi-fredo: whip the egg yolks and coffee extract with a third of the sugar until pale and doubled in size. Lightly whip the cream with another third of the sugar, then whip the egg whites with the remaining sugar. Fold the cream into the sabayon, then fold the egg whites into the mixture. Fill 4 espresso cups two-thirds full and freeze immediately for at least 3 hours. When serving, heat the milk to 50°C and, using a bar blender with a whisk attachment, fluff up the milk and leave it to stand for 2–3 minutes. Spoon on top of the semi-fredo.

For the mocha sorbet: heat up the coffee, syrup and chocolate, stirring constantly until the chocolate is completely dissolved. Pass this through muslin, cool and add the Kahlua.

Serve the dish on an oval plate, placing the tiramisu – lightly dusted with cocoa powder – and the semi-fredo at opposite ends. Position the sorbet in the middle with a slice of lemon for squeezing. At Orrery we set the sorbet on a honey and chocolate tuille as pictured, but a small dish or other small type of biscuit could be used instead.

Paul Gayler
Conservatory Restaurant at The Lanesborough

Paul Gayler
Conservatory Restaurant at The Lanesborough

I have been lucky enough to work in some of London's most respected restaurants over the years. Five years spent working my way up through the ranks at The Royal Garden Hotel led to a couple of years as Sous Chef at the Dorchester, followed by seven years at Inigo Jones.

I think this is really where I made my mark. For years I had been frustrated by the lack of imagination shown by many chefs towards the preparation of vegetarian food. So I tackled the problem head-on with the creation of my *menu potager* – a seven-course gourmet vegetarian dinner, run alongside my à la carte menu. It was an immediate success, earning me the reputation for being the pioneer of vegetarian *haute cuisine*.

In one way or another, the majority of my books have celebrated vegetarian or vegetable cooking, and I was delighted when my *Passion for Vegetables*, published in 1999, was named 'Cookery Book of the Year' by the Guild of Food Writers. I have also enjoyed appearing on numerous TV shows like *Take Six Chefs*, *Open House* and *Food and Drink*, as well as with Richard and Judy on *This Morning*, organising their 'ITV Chef of the Year' programme for the Millennium.

For all this, however, I am still most at home in a busy kitchen, and I joined The Lanesborough in 1991 as part of the team who opened the hotel on New Year's Eve of that year. Here I oversee all the hotel's food preparation with a lively brigade of 40 chefs. We present a Mediterranean style of cuisine with Pacific Rim influences in the Conservatory Restaurant – a menu that indulges my passion for vegetarian cuisine and oriental spices but which still offers unique meat and fish dishes, like the Moroccan-inspired Guinea-fowl and more traditional Braised halibut 'T'-bone that follow.

Paul Gayler
Conservatory Restaurant at The Lanesborough

Tatin of white chicory
with roasted scallops, fumet of orange and basil

for the basil oil
1 bunch of fresh basil
100ml extra virgin olive oil

for the tatins
150g good quality puff pastry,
ready-made
4 Belgian chicory, picked into
leaves
25g salted butter
25g brown sugar

for the orange oil
juice of 3 oranges
zest of 1 orange
25ml Sauternes
60ml walnut oil
60ml extra virgin olive oil
4 basil leaves, coarsely chopped
2 plum tomatoes, peeled,
deseeded and diced
salt and freshly ground black
pepper

other ingredients
12 medium-size scallops, dived
sea salt
freshly ground black pepper
300ml olive oil
4 large basil leaves, deep-fried, to
garnish

For the basil oil: blanch the basil in a pot of boiling water for 30 seconds and refresh with ice-cold water. Drain and dry in a cloth, then place it in a blender with the oil and blitz to a purée. Leave overnight and strain through a sieve before using.

For the tatins: preheat the oven to 190°C (gas mark 5). Roll out the pastry to approximately 3mm thick and cut out four 10cm pastry circles using a cookie cutter. Leave them to rest for 30 minutes in the fridge. Separate the leaves of chicory. Melt the butter in a large frying pan, add the sugar and cook to form a light caramel. Add the chicory leaves and allow them to caramelise for 8–10 minutes to a golden colour and soft consistency. Remove them from the heat and drain.

Arrange the chicory in the base of four 8cm tartlet moulds or blini pans, and top with the pastry circles, ensuring that the outer edge is well tucked in. Place them in the hot oven for 15 minutes, until the pastry is golden and fluffy.

For the orange oil: in a pan bring the orange juice, zest and Sauternes to the boil and reduce by half. Whisk in the oils and form a light emulsion. Add the basil and tomatoes, and season to taste.

To prepare the dish, season the scallops with salt and pepper, and sear for about 30 seconds on each side in a hot pan in olive oil until golden. De-mould the caramelised chicory tatins on to 4 individual serving plates, top each with 3 scallops, pour over the orange oil and drizzle a little basil oil around. Decorate with the fried basil leaves and serve.

Paul Gayler
Conservatory Restaurant at The Lanesborough

Braised halibut 'T'-bone
with spring vegetables and a rosemary-truffle broth

for the vegetables

8 asparagus tips

8 baby violet artichokes

4 tbsp olive oil

juice of 1/2 lemon

12 baby carrots

8 baby turnips

50g sugar snap peas

75g morel mushrooms, cleaned

4 young courgettes

other ingredients

2 tbsp extra virgin olive oil

4 x 175g halibut steaks (bone in)

salt and freshly ground white pepper

20g unsalted butter

1/2 tbsp fresh rosemary

100ml dry white wine

50ml dry vermouth

200ml good quality fish stock

1 tbsp white truffle oil

salt and black pepper

For the vegetables: peel the asparagus and blanch it in boiling water for 2–3 minutes. Then refresh it in iced water, drain and dry. Prepare the artichokes in the normal manner by removing a few of the outer leaves, until you reach the tender, yellowish leaves. Cut off one-third from the top of the artichokes. Heat the olive oil gently, add the artichokes and cook for 1 minute. Add the lemon juice and just cover with water. Poach gently for 6–8 minutes, remove and allow them to cool. In separate pans, blanch the baby carrots, turnips and sugar snaps, refresh in iced water and dry.

Preheat the oven to 190°C (gas mark 5). Heat the olive oil in a high-sided frying pan, season the halibut with salt and pepper, and sear it in the oil for 20 seconds (do not allow it to colour). Add half the butter and rosemary and cook for 4–5 minutes. Pour over the white wine, vermouth and fish stock, bring this to the boil, cover with buttered paper and place in the oven for 4–5 minutes. Remove from the oven, add all the vegetables, re-cover with paper and return to the oven for a further 3–4 minutes, until the fish is cooked.

To prepare the dish, carefully remove the halibut and the vegetables and place into 4 serving bowls. Strain the cooking liquid into a small pan and bring this to the boil. Whisk in the remaining butter and truffle oil and season to taste. Pour the sauce over the fish and vegetables and serve immediately.

Paul Gayler
Conservatory Restaurant at The Lanesborough

Moroccan-inspired guinea fowl

with chard, roasted peppers and olives

4 x 175g breasts of guinea fowl
1 bunch of Swiss chard, picked and
coarsely chopped
2 tbsp olive oil
1 clove of garlic, crushed
1/2 tbsp ground cumin
1/2 tbsp ground coriander
1/2 tbsp grated lemon zest
12 dried apricots, soaked in water
for 1 hour and dried
2 tbsp raisins
4 plum tomatoes, blanched,
deseeded and cut into large pieces
1 red pepper, roasted, skinned and
cut into large pieces
1 tbsp pine kernels, toasted
12 green olives
for the marinade
1 red chilli, deseeded, finely
chopped
2 cloves of garlic, crushed
 juice and zest of 1 lemon
1/2 tbsp ground cinnamon
1 tbsp ground cumin
60ml olive oil
1 tbsp mint, freshly chopped
for the sauce
300ml dark guinea fowl stock
(made from fowl bones)
salt and freshly ground black
pepper
1 tbsp coriander, freshly chopped
1 tbsp mint, freshly chopped

Place the breasts in a shallow dish. Mix together the marinade ingredients and pour over the breasts. Cover and leave to marinate in the fridge for a minimum of 12 hours.

Wash the chard, heat 1 tbsp olive oil in a deep-sided pan, add the garlic and dry spices and cook for 1 minute. Add the chard, lemon zest, apricots and raisins, lower the heat and cook until the chard wilts (12–15 minutes). Add the tomatoes, peppers, pine kernels and olives and cook on for another 5 minutes.

Meanwhile cook the guinea fowl breasts in the remaining oil for around 5 minutes until golden brown. Turn them over, cook the other side and remove them from the heat. Add the prepared stock to the pan and bring it to the boil. Season and add the coriander and mint.

To serve, dress the vegetables on 4 individual serving plates, top with the ginea fowl and pour over the sauce. I like it served with saffron-flavoured couscous as an accompaniment.

Paul Gayler
Conservatory Restaurant at The Lanesborough

Goat's cheese semi-fredo
with tomato and passion fruit sauce

for the tomato crisps
100ml stock syrup
skins from the plum tomatoes

for the semi-fredo
50g caster sugar
2 free-range eggs, separated
1 vanilla pod, seeds removed
200ml double cream
100g soft goat's cheese
zest of 1 orange
75ml light rum
icing sugar to dust
75g cooked meringues, broken
into pieces

for the fruit sauce
1 tbsp unsalted butter
1 tbsp caster sugar
4 firm but ripe plum tomatoes,
blanched, skinned, deseeded and
cut into a small dice
5 passion fruits
1 tbsp kirsch or vodka

For the tomato crisps: bring the stock syrup to the boil, add the tomato skins and leave them to go cold. Remove them from the syrup, place them on a non-stick baking tray and place in a cool oven at 100°F for 4–5 hours until they become crisp. Remove them from the tray and keep them in an airtight container, ready to use.

For the semi-fredo: whisk together the sugar, egg yolks and vanilla seeds in a bowl until pale and doubled in volume. Whip the cream until soft peaks (do not over-whisk). In another bowl, whisk the egg whites until they form very stiff peaks. Add the goat's cheese, orange zest and rum to the egg yolks, mix and blend together. Gently fold in the whipped cream, followed by the egg whites and meringue. Scoop the mixture into your chosen moulds, cover with clingfilm and freeze until ready to use.

For the fruit sauce: heat the butter in a pan with the sugar and caramelise lightly together. Add the tomato, and juice and seeds of the passion fruit. Add the kirsch, cook for 1 minute and keep warm.

To prepare the dish, remove the semi-fredo from the moulds on to individual serving plates and pour over the warm sauce. Decorate with the dried tomato skins, dust with icing sugar and serve.

Fergus Henderson
St John

Fergus Henderson
St John

Seven years at the Architectural Association may not seem the obvious route into running a restaurant but it actually put me in reasonable stead. And with the fickle finger of fate pointing in our direction Jon Spiteri, Trevor Gulliver and I opened St John seven years ago.

Here we have a bar, a bakery and a dining room. So you can stop in for a glass of Madeira and a slice of seed cake, or a Welsh rarebit and a glass of beer, or sit in the dining room and have a grouse and a bottle of claret . . . utilitarian eating and drinking! We are not 'modern British'. Nor are we the thick, sticky and sweet school of cooking which is supposed to give some traditional validity. Instead we use indigenous, seasonal ingredients and cook them well . . . permanent British cooking.

Fergus Henderson
St John

Tripe, sausage and butter beans

for the tripe

1.8kg cleaned tripe, cut into equal, business-card-size pieces
a string of chorizo sausages, about 600g in weight
2 bulbs of garlic, unpeeled
750ml bottle of dry white wine
1 bundle of thyme, tied

for the beans

400g butter beans (soaked overnight in water)
5 bulbs of fennel, sliced thinly against the grain
chicken stock, enough to cover fennel
12 shallots, peeled and sliced
12 cloves of garlic, peeled and chopped
good dollop of duck fat
sea salt and ground black pepper

Put the tripe, chorizo, garlic heads, wine and thyme into a pot and bring them up to a simmer. Cook for approximately 1 hour until the tripe has a giving consistency, but not so giving that it has melted away, then take out the chorizo sausage, chop it up into 1cm thick slices and return the pieces to the pot. Set it aside to cool, but don't refrigerate.

Cook the butter beans in fresh water for approximately 2 hours, checking them occassionally until swollen, soft and giving. Drain them off, then add them to the tripe mixture. Braise the fennel in the stock for around 30 minutes until soft but not pulped, then add it to the pot, and gently fry off the shallots and garlic in the duck fat until translucent, adding these to the pot as well.

Bring the pot back to a simmer for 30–40 minutes so that the ingredients get to know each other, season to taste and serve in a large dish. Serve with much bread for supping up the juices and, of course, plenty of red wine should flow.

Roasted bone marrow

with parsley salad

12 pieces of middle veal
marrowbone, 7–8cm in length
1 bunch of flat-leaf parsley, picked
and lightly chopped
2 shallots, peeled and thinly sliced
1 small handful of capers (extra
fine, if possible)
for the dressing
juice of 1 lemon
extra virgin olive oil
1 pinch of salt and pepper
other ingredients
a good supply of toast
coarse sea salt

This is the one dish that does not change on the menu at St John. The marrow bone comes from a calf's leg, so ask your butcher to keep some for you. You will need a teaspoon or long thin implement to scrape the marrow out of the bone to eat it.

For the bone marrow: preheat the oven to 190°C (gas mark 5) and place the marrowbone in an ovenproof frying pan inside. The roasting process should take about 20 minutes, depending on the thickness of bone. The marrow should be loose and giving, but should not melt away – as it will do if left too long. (Traditionally, the ends would be covered to prevent any seepage, but I like the colouring and crispiness of this part.)

To prepare the dish, mix the parsley with the shallots and capers. Then combine the dressing ingredients and pour this over the salad at the last minute. Remove the marrowbone from the oven – this dish should not be seasoned before leaving the kitchen, as a little coarse sea salt at the moment of eating gives it texture and uplift. So scrape the marrow on to the toast, season it with coarse sea salt, then a pinch of the parsley salad on top of this and eat.

Fergus Henderson
St John

Smoked eel, bacon and mash

Serves 3

1 reasonably large whole smoked eel, or 2 smoked eel fillets cut into 6 pieces

for the mash

2kg floury potatoes (e.g. Maris Piper), peeled and halved
425ml milk
110g unsalted butter
sea salt and ground black pepper

for the bacon

a knob of butter
6 thick rashers of good quality smoked streaky bacon

For the eel: lay it down with its back facing you. With a sharp knife cut behind its head until you feel the backbone, then run the knife along the bone to the tail. Turn it over and repeat the process along its underside. Slip your fingers under the skin and gently run them along each fillet to remove it. Cut both fillets into 3 pieces to give you 6 fillets in all.

For the mash: boil the potatoes in salted water for approximately 30 minutes until soft when stabbed with a knife. Heat up the milk and butter, add them to the drained potatoes and mash. Season to taste, remembering that the bacon is quite salty.

For the bacon: heat up a frying pan and add a knob of butter. Place the bacon slices in the pan and cook to taste and preference of crispiness. When cooked, remove the bacon and keep it warm. Place the eel fillets in the pan, giving them a few moments' cooking either side in the butter and fat that the bacon should have released.

To serve, place the eel on the mashed potato and top it with 2 slices of bacon, pouring the remaining bacon and eel fat from the frying pan over the top.

St John's Eccles cake

for the puff pastry*

125g unsalted butter (butter A),
cold from the fridge
500g strong white flour
1 pinch of sea salt
250ml water
375g unsalted butter (butter B),
cold from the fridge

for the filling

50g unsalted butter
110g dark brown sugar
220g currants
1 tsp ground allspice
1 tsp ground nutmeg

for the glaze

3 egg whites, beaten with a fork
a shallow bowl of caster sugar

*NOTE: this recipe should easily
make a dozen cakes. If you have
pastry left over, it freezes well.

Oddly enough for a restaurant with a certain carnivorous reputation, we serve a vegetarian Eccles cake – omitting to use the traditional lard in the pastry and using puff pastry instead. So apologies to the traditional cake-bakers of Eccles, but this recipe is delicious, particularly when consumed with Lancashire cheese.

For the puff pastry: do not be daunted by this recipe. It is quite simple in practice. Mix butter A with the flour and salt using your fingers, until the mixture resembles breadcrumbs, then cautiously add the water and mix until you have a firm paste. Pat this into a square, wrap it in clingfilm and leave it to rest in the fridge for at least 1 hour before using.

Once rested, roll the paste into a rectangle about 8mm thick. Then beat butter B between greaseproof paper into a rectangle that is about half the size of the paste rectangle. Lay the butter on the paste, leaving a space at the end. Fold the unbuttered half over the butter and fold the edges over so that the butter is in a paste package. Pat the square down, wrap it in clingfilm, and allow it to rest in the fridge for at least 15 minutes. Then roll it out into a rectangle in the opposite direction to your initial major fold. Each time you roll out the pastry to fold it, turn the pastry and roll across the previous direction you rolled in. Sprinkle flour on the surface of your rolling pin, but make sure you dust the flour off the pâté before folding it at every turn in the process. Once the pastry is approximately 1–1½cm thick, fold it like a traditional letter – with one end of the rectangle to the halfway mark and the other end over this. Pat the square down and place it in the fridge for at least 15 minutes to rest again. Repeat this process two more times but no more! This is essential for successful puff pastry. Return it to the fridge to rest for 1 hour or more.

For the filling: melt the butter and sugar together, then add them to the dry ingredients, mix well and then leave them to cool before using.

For the Eccles cake: preheat the oven to 200°C (gas mark 6). Roll out the puff pastry to 7–8mm thick and cut out circles about 9cm in diameter. Spoon a small amount of the filling mixture on to the centre of half of these, then place the other pastry circles on top. Pinch the edges together, gently pressing to flatten the cakes, then slash the top 3 times (I'm told it is very significant how many times an Eccles cake is slashed).

For the glaze: paint the top with the egg white, then dip it into the sugar. Bake them in the oven for 15–20 minutes, making sure they don't burn. Serve them either hot or cold with some Lancashire cheese.

Chris McGowan
Searcy's at the Barbican

Chris McGowan
Searcy's at the Barbican

Like most boys at school, sport was my abiding passion. But when I was fourteen my mother persuaded me to take a summer and weekend job helping in the kitchen of a restaurant that she managed, and that's where my desire to know more about cooking began to grow.

On leaving school I combined part-time study with full-time employment at a local hotel. After a couple of years I finished my course and went to work at the Ramore Restaurant in Portrush with George McAlpin – easily the best chef in Northern Ireland at the time. I stayed there for five years, and then moved to London to start work at the newly opened L'Odeon Restaurant in Regent Street, where I stayed for eleven months.

I then spent four years with Gary Rhodes – first at The Greenhouse and later as his Sous Chef at City Rhodes – before working with Pierre Koffman at La Tante Claire as Senior Sous Chef. And that brings me to my present position as Executive Head Chef here at Searcy's at the Barbican. The restaurant itself has an excellent view of the courtyard and fountains of St Giles Church, and our aim is to satisfy the art-loving clientele, the neighbourhood businesses and the residential community that lives on site.

Our menu offers a sturdy balance of modern British food with French influences. The love of offal and earthy ingredients can be seen in dishes like Braised Pigs' Trotters with Black Pudding, or perhaps Tea-smoked Salmon with Spiced Cabbage. Some of the dishes I have selected for this book are also on the menu at The Barbican – dishes like the roasted scallops, for example, where the earthy flavours of the carrot purée and crispy pork balance the rich texture of the scallops. On the other hand I love making the lamb dish because it allows me to use every part of the animal, while the pan-fried halibut is a great summer dish that combines the distinctive flavour of smoked eel with the meatiness of the fish, and with apple bringing the whole dish together. The dessert also draws together a variety of different textures – the warm spiced pear, the creaminess of the pyramid brûlée and the light crispiness of the cinnamon beignet filled with warm pear. A delight created by Paul Gregory our Pastry Chef.

Roast scallops
with crispy pork carrots

for the pork

1 large pork belly (4–5kg)
10g unsalted butter
4 onions, sliced
1/2 head of celery, sliced
1 star anise
3 cardamom seed
10g fresh ginger, chopped
2 cloves of garlic, crushed
1/3 bunch of fresh thyme
1/3 bunch of marjoram
900ml chicken stock
600ml port
125g blossom honey
2 cups soy sauce
20ml balsamic vinegar (8-year-old)

for the carrot purée

5 large carrots
25g unsalted butter
1 tsp demerara sugar
2 star anise
2 cardamom seeds, crushed
double cream
salt and white pepper

for the butter sauce

8 baby carrots
20ml Gewürztraminer white wine
25ml double cream
25g unsalted butter
salt and white pepper

other ingredients

unsalted butter
balsamic vinegar, 20-year-old
vegetable oil
salt and white pepper
1 bunch of chervil, chopped

For the pork: soak the pork belly overnight in water. Preheat the oven to 110°C. Melt a little of the butter in a pan and caramelise the onions and celery. Place the pork belly skin-side down in a separate pan and seal it on all sides. When coloured, add it to the onions and celery along with the star anise, 3 cardamom seeds, and the ginger, garlic and herbs. Then add the chicken stock, port, honey, soy sauce and balsamic vinegar and braise the pork slowly in the oven for 2–2½ hours. When cooked, remove it from the pan and press it down with heavy weights overnight.

For the carrot purée: cook the large carrots in water with the butter and sugar, along with the star anise and cardamom seeds. When cooked, take the carrots out – reserving the cooking liquor – and purée them to a smooth paste. Add a touch of cream, season to taste, and pass through a fine sieve.

For the butter sauce: place the baby carrots in the reserved carrot stock and cook for 5–6 minutes until soft. Remove the carrots, keeping them warm on one side, and reduce the liquor by half. Add the Gewürztraminer, reduce again by half, then add the cream and reduce by a third. Whisk in the butter, season it to taste, then pass the sauce through a fine sieve.

To prepare the dish, slice the pork belly lengthways and caramelise it in a little butter. Deglaze the pan with a splash of balsamic vinegar and set it aside. Roast the scallops in a little vegetable oil, caramelising them on one side for 2–3 minutes until they are golden brown, before turning them over and sealing them on the other side. Leave them to rest for 1–2 minutes.

To serve, warm through the carrot purée and place a large teardrop on a plate. Place the pork beside this, with the scallops on top. Warm through the baby carrots in a little butter, season them lightly and arrange these around the plate. Then warm the butter sauce through, add the chervil at the last minute, check the seasoning and serve around the scallops.

Chris McGowan
Searcy's at the Barbican

Pan-fried halibut

with celeriac purée, smoked eel and apple tortellinis

for the curry oil
15ml apple juice
50ml olive oil
1 tsp mild curry powder

for the purée
1 large celeriac, peeled and diced
juice of 1 lemon
125g unsalted butter
double cream (optional)
salt and white pepper

for the tortellinis
5–6 small strands of saffron
1 tbsp water
1kg Italian flour
8 eggs
100ml olive oil
200g smoked eel, finely diced
2 baby gem lettuce, thinly sliced
1 Granny Smith apple, finely sliced
and cut into strips
1 tbsp fresh coriander, finely
chopped
salt and white pepper

for the halibut
1 x 175g halibut fillet per person
125g unsalted butter
salt and white pepper

for the salad
100g green salad leaves
200g fresh herbs (chives, chervil,
tarragon and coriander)
25ml olive oil
25ml vegetable oil
squeeze of lemon juice
salt and white pepper

For the curry oil: reduce the apple juice by two-thirds in a pan and allow to cool. Then mix it into the olive oil together with the curry powder, allowing the flavours to infuse for 30 minutes.

For the purée: melt the butter in a pan over a low heat, add the celeriac, lemon juice and seasoning, and cook gently for 25 minutes. Blend in a liquidiser, check the seasoning and add a touch of cream if needed. Set aside until required.

For the tortellinis: infuse the saffron in the water on a stove for 2–3 minutes. Sift the dry ingredients into a bowl and make a well in the middle. Add the egg, olive oil and saffron water, and knead into a soft dough. Cover the bowl with clingfilm and leave it to rest in the fridge for 1 hour. While the dough is resting, mix the smoked eel, lettuce and apple chiffonade together with half the coriander and season to taste. Roll out the pasta dough very thinly and cut it into 50mm circles. Place a little eel mixture in the centre and overlap the sides, sticking them with a little water. Finally stick the two ends together and repeat until the dough is finished.

For the halibut: lightly butter the fish and place it in a hot pan. Colour it well for 4 minutes on one side, turn it over to seal the other, before seasoning it and leaving it to rest for 2 minutes.

For the salad: mix the salad leaves and fresh herbs together with the olive oil and lemon juice, seasoning to taste.

To prepare the dish, place the tortellinis into seasoned boiling water and cook for about 3 minutes. Meanwhile, place the curry oil and remaining chopped coriander into a separate pan and, when the tortellinis are ready, remove them from the water and coat them really well in the oil.

To serve, put a large spoonful of celeriac purée on to each plate with a halibut fillet on top. Arrange 5 tortellini around the edge, pour the remainder of the curry oil over the fish and arrange the salad neatly on top.

Chris McGowan
Searcy's at the Barbican

Assiette of Pyrenees lamb

1 8kg Pyrenees lamb
olive oil
salt and white pepper
1 litre lamb stock

for the herb crust
breadcrumbs from 1/2 a stale loaf
100g fresh flat-leaf parsley, finely
chopped
1/3 bunch of fresh marjoram, finely
chopped
1 tsp Dijon mustard, to coat the
rack

for the stuffing
minced lamb trimmings
2 egg yolks
90g red pepper, roasted and diced
45g black olives, pitted and
chopped

for the faggot farce
2 carrots, peeled and sliced
1 onion, peeled and sliced
10g unsalted butter
1 savoy cabbage

for the fillet etc.
1 tsp olive oil
570ml vegetable oil for deep-frying
250g self-raising flour
1 bottle of lager
salt and white pepper

for the sauce
1 litre reserved lamb stock
a knob of unsalted butter
10g red pepper, roasted and diced
5g black olives, pitted and
chopped
salt and white pepper

Bone out the lamb leaving only the saddle intact. When the shoulders are boned, season them and lay them under clingfilm. Beat them out and roll them into a cylinder, tying it with string. Colour this in a pan in 1 tsp olive oil, then sear the neck and braise both for 1 1/2 hours in the lamb stock. Cut the saddle into racks and clean up all the bones, then season the legs of lamb, place them under clingfilm and beat them out too.

For the leg stuffing: preheat the grill, until it is very hot, and place the red pepper under it until the skin has blackened. Remove it and place it in clingfilm until it has cooled. Peel off the skin and dice. Combine the breadcrumbs, parsley and marjoram, and place 175g in a mixing bowl, reserving 25g for the rack of lamb. Mix the herb crust with 90g of the diced pepper and all of the other stuffing ingredients, and season. Place the stuffing in the centre of the legs, roll them up then tie them securely, leaving them in the fridge until required.

For the shoulder: when the shoulder is braised, remove it from the stock, cut the string and leave it to cool. Roll it tightly in clingfilm, tying it at both ends and leave it to rest in the fridge.

For the faggot farce: when the neck is braised, reserve the stock for the sauce, and take all the meat from the bone. Reserve the leaves from the cabbage and shred the heart. Caramelise the carrots and onions in the butter and after 5 minutes add the shredded cabbage with 1 tbsp of water. Steam until tender, season, then add the neck meat. Divide the mixture into 4 and wrap each tightly with cabbage leaves, setting them aside until needed.

For the fillet, kidney, liver and sweetbread: mix the seasoned flour and lager together into a batter, and leave it to rest in the fridge for 1 hour. Sear the kidneys, liver and fillet in the olive oil for 2–2 1/2 minutes and allow to rest. Dust the sweetbreads in a little flour, coat them in the batter and deep-fry them in the vegetable oil for 3–4 minutes until golden brown.

For the sauce: reduce the stock by half, stir in the knob of butter, and add the red peppers and olives. Season to taste and keep warm until needed. To prepare the dish, preheat the oven to 200°C (gas mark 6). Slice the shoulder into 50–60g pieces and reheat them in the lamb sauce. Slice up the stuffed leg, pan-fry it in a little olive oil and cook it in the oven for 4–5 minutes, before leaving it to rest. Pan-fry the rack of lamb in a little olive oil, then brush it with a smear of mustard and sprinkle it with the remaining herb crust. Steam the faggots for 3–4 minutes, arrange all the components on the plate and drizzle the remaining sauce around the edge to serve.

Chris McGowan
Searcy's at the Barbican

Poached pear

with a pyramid of crème brûlée and cinnamon beignets

for the pears

2 litres red wine

500g caster sugar

100g soft brown sugar

2 cinnamon sticks

40g star anise

2 vanilla pods, split lengthways

20g juniper berries

8g cloves

5 baby pears

for the crème brûlée

500ml double cream

1 vanilla pod, split lengthways

125g caster sugar

7 egg yolks

for the cinnamon beignet

250g water

250g milk

160g unsalted butter

4g salt

30g caster sugar

300g plain flour

400g egg

570ml vegetable oil

other ingredients

10ml double cream, lightly whipped

25g ground cinnamon

25g ground caster sugar

For the pears: place 1 litre of red wine with all the other ingredients apart from the baby pears in a pan and reduce over a low heat by half. Add the rest of the red wine, place the baby pears in the pan, and cook over a low flame for about 1 hour. When cooked, remove the pan from the heat, and place a bowl over the pears while still in the hot stock. This will stop them from rising to the surface. Leave in the stock for at least 48 hours before use.

For the crème brûlée: bring the cream and vanilla pod to the boil in a thick-bottomed pan. Meanwhile, whisk together the sugar and the yolks until pale. Pour half the boiled cream over the egg mixture while whisking, then pour this back into the rest of the cream and allow it to cool. Pour the mixture into a $1/4$ gallon container and rest it in the fridge for 24 hours. Preheat the oven to 100°C. Pour the mixture into 8 pyramid moulds, sit them in a bain-marie and cook them in the oven for 1 hour. Leave them to cool for about 20 minutes, and place them back in the fridge again until required.

For the cinnamon beignet: place all the ingredients, apart from the flour, eggs and oil, into a thick-bottomed pan and boil quickly. Remove the pan from the heat, whisk in the flour, and put it back on the heat again to cook for 10 minutes. Place the mixture in an electric mixer and beat until cool. Slowly add the eggs and beat until all are fully combined. Place the mixture into a piping bag with a 1cm nozzle and pipe 2cm lengths into the hot cooking oil. Remove them from the oil with a slotted spoon once golden brown and drain them on kitchen paper. Remove one of the pears from the poaching stock and purée it with a little of the poaching liquor and the lightly whipped cream. Carefully pipe this into the warm beignets, then mix the ground cinnamon and caster sugar together, and roll the beignet in it.

To serve, reduce 570ml of the poaching liquor by two-thirds. Place the pears in this, turning them after 1 minute. Place the pear in one corner of the plate, with the crème brûlée opposite and the beignets at the top corner, carefully spooning the reduced stock around two sides of the plate.

Paul Merrett
The Greenhouse

Paul Merrett
The Greenhouse

Alex Ferguson never called, so I became a chef. Sure, life as a football superstar would have been OK, but I think I made the right decision. I have always loved eating, and luckily that passion lends itself readily to cooking.

My wife MJ calls me obsessive, but I prefer dedicated enthusiast. After my apprenticeship at The Ritz, I moved to Le Soufflé to work for Peter Kromberg – a man whose influence still affects my culinary philosophy. My next stop was three years in Mayfair at The Greenhouse under Gary Rhodes.

I then moved to The Terrace Restaurant in Piccadilly to take up my first position as head chef, allowing me the freedom to experiment and express the ideas that now are the basis of my repertoire. A short spell at the Mount Lavinia Hotel in Sri Lanka was followed in October 1997 by an exciting spell at The Interlude in London's Charlotte Street, where we received many rave reviews and I was awarded my first Michelin star – a strangely poignant moment.

On the back of this, the big time came knocking. Joseph Levin, owner of The Greenhouse, contacted me with a challenge – to take the restaurant back to the premiere league. Newly refurbished, we reopened in October 2001. The Greenhouse is now a light, elegant room with a fresh modern interior that is both striking and beautiful. My menu is a mix of classic flavours and spicy innovation. The result – come and see for yourself.

for the lamb

50g coriander seeds

50g cumin seeds

4 tbsp olive oil

4 x 175g pieces of lamb loin

for the lamb jus

approx. 1kg lamb bones, chopped (ask the butcher for the bones from which the loin was taken)

4 sprigs of fresh thyme

4 sprigs of fresh rosemary

1 pinch of saffron

2 star anise

1 dried chilli, whole

1 onion, peeled and chopped

2 cloves of garlic, roughly chopped

2.25 litres lamb stock (or cubes)

1 red pepper, roasted in the oven, skinned and finely diced

8 basil leaves, diced

1 tbsp pine nuts, roasted and chopped in half

for the aubergine confit

1 aubergine, peeled and diced (2cm)

2 tbsp olive oil

1 onion, peeled and chopped

2 cloves of garlic, peeled and chopped

1 sprig of fresh thyme

1 sprig of fresh rosemary

salt and milled white pepper

for the sweet potatoes

4 orange-flesh sweet potatoes, peeled and cut into cylinders

1 tbsp olive oil

for the aubergine roll

1 onion, peeled and chopped

2 tsp olive oil

200g button mushrooms, sliced

190ml dry white wine

100ml fresh tomato juice

4 thin slices of aubergine, cut lengthways

other ingredients

200g spinach leaves

Cumin roasted loin of lamb

with sweet potato sauté, aubergine confit and spiced lamb jus

This is a complex selection of simple dishes, some of which should be started well in advance.

For the lamb: dry-fry the coriander and cumin seeds in a pan, then cool and grind them up, mixing them into a paste with the olive oil. Rub this into the lamb, and allow it to marinate for 2–3 days.

For the lamb jus: roast the lamb bones in a saucepan in a little vegetable oil until golden in colour, then add all the herbs, spices, onion, garlic and the lamb stock, and allow to simmer for 2 hours or until the liquor has reduced to just 600ml. Pour the juice through a fine sieve and set it on one side until needed.

For the aubergine confit: preheat the oven to 140°C (gas mark 1). In a lidded, ovenproof pan, fry the diced aubergine in the olive oil with the chopped onion, garlic and herbs for 5 minutes and season it with salt and pepper. Put the lid on and cook it slowly in the oven for 1 hour until the aubergine is soft. Place the mixture on one side until needed.

For the sweet potatoes: cook the sweet potato cylinders in boiling salted water until cooked but still firm. Allow them to cool, then cut the cylinders into 2cm thick slices and set them on one side until needed.

For the aubergine and mushroom roll: sweat off the onion in the olive oil until they are soft but not coloured. Add the sliced button mushrooms and cook on for 2 minutes, before adding the wine and reducing the mixture until dry. Repeat this process with the tomato juice, then allow the mixture to cool. Paint the aubergine slices with olive oil and place them into a hot ribbed pan until the slices become marked with the lines of the pan. Then place a quarter of the cooled aubergine and mushroom mixture on to one end and roll the aubergine slice up. Set the rolls on one side until needed. To prepare the dish, preheat the oven to 180°C (gas mark 4) and roast the marinated lamb for 6 minutes or until pink in the centre, before allowing it to rest for 5 minutes. Warm through the lamb jus, add the red peppers, basil and pine nuts, and pan-fry the sweet potato in the olive oil until golden brown. Reheat the aubergine and mushroom rolls in the microwave for one minute, warm through the aubergine confit in a pan and cook the spinach in boiling salted water for 20 seconds, before draining it and setting it on one side. To serve, lay the sweet potato slices in a circle on the plate, and fill the centre with cooked spinach. Place a spoonful of aubergine confit on top of the spinach and lay the carved lamb on top. Pour the lamb jus neatly around and finish with the aubergine roll on top.

Crab mayonnaise

with new potato dauphine, mango and pepper vinaigrette

1 medium cock crab, cooked*
300ml good rich mayonnaise, readymade (homemade is by far the best, however)
milled white pepper

for the choux pastry
110g unsalted butter
275ml water
salt
225g plain flour, sifted
6 eggs, beaten
20 new potatoes, peeled and cooked
570ml vegetable oil

for the pepper vinaigrette
1 red pepper, deseeded and cut into small pieces
1 red chilli, deseeded and cut into small pieces
1/2 clove of garlic, crushed
1 pinch of saffron
1/2 tbsp caster sugar
salt and milled white pepper
up to 8 tbsp olive oil

other ingredients
1 ripe mango
a little aged balsamic vinegar
4 sprigs chervil to garnish

For the crab: pick through the crab to remove any pieces of shell, then mix it with just enough mayonnaise to enrich but not overpower the crab's flavour. Refrain from adding any salt, but add just a little milled pepper.

For the choux pastry: bring the butter and water to the boil with a pinch of salt in a pan. As soon as it reaches boiling point, add the flour and stir with a spoon over the heat until the mixture comes away from the sides. Allow this to cool to blood temperature, then gradually mix in the eggs. Crush the potatoes with a fork and mix them with the choux pastry – two-thirds potato to one-third choux pastry – spooning this into an 8cm round cutter on silicon paper. Remove the cutter and chill in the fridge until needed, repeating this process until you have made four.

For the mango: peel off the skin from the mango and remove all the flesh, puréeing it in a blender and leaving it on one side until needed.

For the pepper vinaigrette: gently fry the pepper and chilli for 3 minutes with the garlic, saffron, sugar, salt and pepper. Purée the mixture in a blender whilst adding a little olive oil to emulsify the vinaigrette.

To prepare the dish, deep-fry the potato dauphines in vegetable oil for 4 minutes until golden brown. Place one in the centre of each plate, position a small cutter on top and fill it with the crab mayonnaise. Remove the cutter, spoon the pepper vinaigrette and mango purée around the edge with a little balsamic vinegar, garnish with a sprig of chervil and serve.

*NOTE: bought, pre-prepared cooked-in-the-shell crabs, or ready prepared unpasteurised white meat will both give good flavour. Far superior, however, is a recently caught live specimen, which should be boiled immediately for 8 minutes, removed from the liquid and cooled.

Paul Merrett
The Greenhouse

Pan-fried fillet of halibut

with clam and bacon stew

for the halibut

4 x 175g portions of halibut, skin removed*

a little unsalted butter, melted

plain flour for dusting

1tbsp olive oil

for the stew

1 onion, diced (4cm)

6 rashers of streaky bacon, cut across into 3cm dice

2 tbsp olive oil

150g girolle mushroom (any wild mushroom could be substituted)

2 cloves of garlic, crushed

1 tbsp fresh thyme, picked

salt and milled white pepper

20 Parlourde clams

275ml chicken stock, hot

1 large savoy cabbage, roughly diced

150ml double cream

For the halibut: prior to cooking, lightly brush the presentation side (side that has no skin) of the fish with a little soft butter and dust it with flour to protect the flesh from the heat of the pan. Pan-fry it for 3–4 minutes on each side (presentation side down first) in the olive oil until golden brown.

For the stew: pan-fry the onion and bacon in the olive oil until golden brown. Add the girolles, garlic, thyme and seasoning, and cook for a further 2 minutes. Then throw in the clams and stock, cover the pan with a lid and cook over a high heat until the clams open their shells. Remove the lid, add the uncooked cabbage and cream, cook for 2 minutes then serve immediately with the halibut on top.

*NOTE: most salt-water fish – especially brill, cod or hake – can be substituted according to price, season and availability.

Plum 'tarte fin'

with yoghurt, black pepper and lemon grass ice-cream
and plum sauce

for the ice-cream

400g milk

400g caster sugar

25g glucose

2 sticks of lemon grass, chopped

400g Greek yoghurt

100g double cream

12 tbsp cracked black pepper

for the frangipan

100g unsalted butter

100g icing sugar

35g plain flour

100g ground almonds

2 eggs and 1 extra yolk, lightly
beaten

for the tart

500g puff pastry, readymade

8 plums, stoned and sliced

for the sauce

4 plums, stoned and chopped

4 tsp caster sugar

For the ice-cream: boil up the milk, sugar, glucose and lemon grass and allow the mixture to infuse for 2 minutes, before cooling it and removing the lemon grass. Whisk in the yoghurt and cream, add a little cracked black pepper, and churn in a sorbetière.

For the frangipan: beat together the butter and icing sugar until very white and creamy, then fold in the flour and almonds and gradually add the eggs. Refrigerate the frangipani until it is firm.

For the tart: roll out the pastry until it is about 3mm thick. Prick it with a fork and cut it into four 18cm discs, before allowing it to rest in the fridge for 1 hour. Preheat the oven to 180°C (gas mark 4), then spread a tablespoon of frangipan over the pastry, with a circular fan of the sliced plums on top. Dust with a little more icing sugar, then bake in the oven for 20 minutes or until the pastry is golden brown.

For the sauce: mix the chopped plums with the sugar and cook in a pan over a gentle heat. The plums will release a lot of natural juice and this should be reduced down completely (stirring with a wooden spoon to avoid sticking) in order to allow the plums to reabsorb these tasty juices. When completely reduced, blend the mixture in a food mixer.

To serve, place the warm tart in the centre of the plate. Spoon the plum sauce around the edge and place a ball of ice-cream on the top. At The Greenhouse we finish the dish with a caramelised sugar spiral. At home, however, I finish the dish with a less time-consuming sprig of mint.

John Newton
Teatro

John Newton
Teatro

I always wanted to become a chef when I was young, and luckily my parents were extremely supportive. I got myself a weekend job while I was at school, making salads and washing pots in a local fish restaurant, and then spent three years at Runshaw College in Lancashire, with placements at The Old Course Hotel in St Andrews and The Walnut Tree in South Wales.

Teatro, owned by Lee Chapman and Leslie Ash, opened in February 1998, and I initially came on board in the August of that year as Sous Chef. We are situated on Shaftsbury Avenue in the heart of London's theatre district and, because of this, many people come here for our unique, pre-show menu. Now, in the wrong hands, a meal eaten with the clock ticking and the curtain due to go up, could easily turn into a mad scramble. Not here. We deliberately foster a relaxed and inviting atmosphere, and a strict no mobile phones and no cameras policy applies, no matter who you are – something I know that our customers really appreciate.

Our food is modern European in style and we offer a wide-ranging menu based on fresh and seasonal produce. Take the Manouri cheese on the following pages, for example – the perfect summer dish and one that contrasts entirely with the pork. And what could be more simple than an organic chop grilled with an apple jus – although watch out for the home-made black pudding. Not for the faint-hearted!

John Newton
Teatro

Warm Manouri cheese

with pine nuts and rocket salad

for the pesto

1 bunch of basil

50g Parmesan cheese, grated

1 clove of garlic, crushed

150ml olive oil

30g pinenuts, toasted

salt and black pepper

for the salad

200g Manouri cheese

30ml olive oil

salt and black pepper

200g rocket, washed and picked

80g pinenuts, toasted

For the pesto: blend all ingredients together in a food processor, then season and chill in an airtight container.

For the salad: cut the Manouri cheese into 4 equal portions using a hot knife. Preheat a cast-iron griddle, and season and lightly oil the slices of Manouri. Carefully place the cheese on the griddle, turning after about 15 seconds, and then allow it to cool.

To prepare the dish, dress the rocket in a small amount of pesto, and divide it between 4 plates. Place the slices of Manouri next to the rocket, finish with more of the pesto and garnish with the pinenuts.

John Newton
Teatro

Steamed fillet of sea bass
with slow-roasted vine tomatoes and asparagus

400g medium-sized asparagus
4 x 200g sea bass fillets, cleaned
and scaled
salt and black pepper

for the tomatoes
12 ripe plum tomatoes, cored and
halved
2 cloves of garlic, peeled and thinly
sliced
1 small bunch of thyme, picked
sea salt and black pepper

for the salsa verde
30g fresh chervil
30g fresh tarragon
30g fresh flat-leaf parsley
200ml extra virgin olive oil
25g capers
1 tbsp Dijon mustard

For the tomatoes: preheat the oven to its lowest setting. Place the tomatoes on a stainless-steel tray, with the garlic, thyme, sea salt and black pepper on top. Place them in the oven for about 4 hours or until soft.

For the salsa verde: place the herbs and olive oil in a food processor and blend to a coarse dressing, before gently folding in the capers and Dijon mustard.

For the asparagus: trim the very bottom of each piece of asparagus and peel each length, removing the tough outer skin. Immerse them in salted boiling water and cook for 4–5 minutes until soft.

For the sea bass: check that all the bones and scales have been removed from the sea bass, then cut through each fillet to give two equal halves. Liberally season each half, then place the tail piece underneath, creating a 'sandwich'. Wrap each fillet tightly in clingfilm and steam for approximately 8 minutes.

To prepare the dish, arrange the tomatoes and asparagus on each plate then carefully remove the clingfilm from the sea bass and serve dressed with the salsa verde.

Gloucester Old Spot pork chop

with black pudding and apple jus

for the apple jus
1 litre apple juice
250g unsalted butter, diced

for the mashed potatoes
500g Maris Piper potatoes
100ml double cream, warmed
100g salted butter

other ingredients
2 Granny Smith apples, peeled,
cored and cut into 6 wedges
75g caster sugar
salt and black pepper
4 pork chops
2 tbsp vegetable oil
4 slices of black pudding

At Teatro we produce our own black pudding, but this can prove time-consuming and it is not easy to reproduce in small quantities. Therefore, I would recommend purchasing it from a quality butcher.

For the apple jus: place the apple juice in a small saucepan and gently reduce to a light caramel, taking care not to burn the sides of the pan. Gradually whisk in the butter, remove from the heat but do not allow to cool.

For the mashed potatoes: prepare the mash in the usual way, adding the warm cream and butter once the potato is smooth.

To prepare the dish, cover the apple wedges with the caster sugar and quickly toss them in a very hot frying pan, turning the apples golden brown. Season the pork chops and cook them on a hot grill for 10–12 minutes, turning occasionally. Meanwhile, heat up a little vegetable oil in a hot frying pan and gently sear the black pudding on both sides. Once coloured, reduce the heat and allow it to cook through for 4 minutes. Arrange all the ingredients on plates and serve immediately.

Summer fruit soup

with vanilla ice-cream

for the syrup
juice of 1 lemon
500ml water
250g caster sugar
1 cinnamon stick

for the soup
zest of 1 orange
zest of 1 lemon
1 punnet of ripe strawberries,
cleaned and stalked
1 punnet of wild strawberries,
cleaned and stalked
4 scoops of vanilla ice-cream

For the syrup: place all the ingredients in a saucepan and bring them to the boil, simmering for about 30 minutes. Remove it from the heat, allow to cool, and pass the syrup through a fine sieve.

For the soup: bring the syrup to the boil with the orange and lemon zest. Place the strawberries in a large bowl, cover them with the boiling syrup and leave them to cool.

Divide the soup between 4 bowls and serve with vanilla ice-cream.

Curtis Stone
Quo Vadis

Curtis Stone
Quo Vadis

What attracted me to Quo Vadis was primarily its location. Soho is a place of extremes – darkness and sleaze; glamour and culture. It has been famous for its eateries since the late 1800s, and Quo Vadis itself has been one of London's most sought-after restaurants since its opening in 1926.

It has had an amazing history and taken many turns over the last 75 years. Karl Marx used to live here, and previous owners have included Peppino Leoni, Damien Hirst and today Marco Pierre White. To say that it is an incredibly creative environment with an amazing aura, therefore, is an understatement, and today its slick and contemporary dining room boasts original exhibits by Andy Warhol and Marco himself.

In a way, I see my food as contemporary art too and so I cannot imagine a better place in which to serve it. I concentrate on flavours with a modern Italian/Mediterranean edge – a far cry from my mother's baking and grandma's divine fudge that inspired me all those years ago back in Australia. But what really got me going when I was fifteen was seeing the pressure chefs endure and watching them push themselves to the absolute limit. So I began to cook at The Savoy Hotel in my home town of Melbourne.

I have always been an extremist. In the kitchen my obsessive nature is let loose. It's a place where I can be passionate – where I can stand for 16 hours a day, six days a week until I achieve perfection. All or nothing. Who wants compromise? But any chef de cuisine is only as good as his team, and my Sous Chef, Chris Haworth, is as good a partner as I could ever hope to have.

It is so important to sit down and take your time to eat, drink and enjoy. Your favourite food. Your favourite wine. Your favourite friends. Perfection!

Carpaccio of beef

with sauce cipriani

250g fillet of beef

for the sauce

2 egg yolks

30ml lemon juice

20ml white wine vinegar

1/2 tsp Dijon mustard

2 anchovy fillets

25ml Worcestershire sauce

235ml olive oil

50ml milk

salt and cracked black pepper

Carpaccio can be made in a hundred different ways. This is the original method from Harry's Bar in Venice and I think it is the best.

For the sauce: place all the ingredients, except the oil and milk, in a food processor. Blitz it at a high speed, adding the oil in a slow but constant stream. Once all the oil is incorporated, add the milk until you achieve the desired consistency. Season with freshly cracked pepper and salt.

For the beef: slice the raw beef very thinly with a very sharp knife, pressing the slices out on the plate to ensure it is wafer thin.

To serve, place the slice of beef on a plate and drizzle the sauce over the top.

Tagliatelle of crab and sea scallops

with chilli oil

1kg fresh tagliatelle
3 shallots, finely diced
4 cloves of garlic, crushed
1 fresh chilli, chopped
100ml extra virgin olive oil
200g crab meat, picked
100ml white wine
12 scallops
5 tomatoes, skinned, deseeded and diced
a pinch of fresh parsley, chopped
deep-fried basil leaves
olive oil
lemon juice

This is such a quick recipe, you can prepare the dish while your pasta is cooking. Fresh tagliatelle can be purchased from any good Italian deli and will take 1–2 minutes to cook.

Cook the pasta in boiling salted water. Cook the shallots, chilli and garlic on a medium heat in 50ml of the olive oil for 2 minutes so that they are softened but not coloured. Add the picked crab and, after 30 seconds, deglaze the pan with the white wine. Shake the excess water from the pasta and add it to the crab. Meanwhile, sear the scallops in the remaining oil in another hot pan for 1 minute on each side. Drop the basil leaves into hot olive oil for 15 seconds to deep-fry them – be careful as they may spit! Then toss the pasta with the tomatoes and parsley, and add a dash of extra virgin olive oil to finish.

To prepare the dish, push a carving fork through the centre of the tagliatelle and twist it so that the pasta is curled around. Remove the scallops from the heat and add a few drops of lemon. Untwist the pasta on to the plate and place the scallops around. Garnish with the deep-fried basil and a drizzle of olive oil.

If desired, chilli oil can be made by simply infusing a few hot chillies with good extra virgin olive oil for 4–5 weeks. This is lovely for drizzling over the pasta.

Roast rump of lamb
with clams and gremolata

for the gremolata

1 bunch of parsley, finely chopped
5 cloves of garlic, crushed
zest of 2 lemons, 2 limes and 1
orange, finely chopped
50ml extra virgin olive oil
sea salt

for the lamb

500g fresh borlotti beans
500ml fresh chicken stock (now
readily available from
supermarkets)
4 rumps new season lamb
50ml olive oil
1 shallot, finely chopped
2 cloves of garlic, crushed
40 Palourdes clams
50ml dry white wine
30g fresh flat-leaf parsley, chopped
salt and black pepper to taste
200g good quality chorizo sausage

For the gremolata: mix all the ingredients together and leave them in the fridge for 5–6 hours.

For the lamb: cook the borlotti beans for about $1^{1}/_{2}$ hours in the chicken stock until they are soft but not broken up. Preheat the oven to its hottest setting. Seal all sides of the lamb rump in a hot pan in 20ml of the olive oil, then roast it in the oven in the same pan for 8 minutes until it is pink. Sauté the shallots and garlic in 30ml olive oil in another very hot pan, and add the clams, white wine and parsley. Drain the beans and toss them with some olive oil and seasoning. Remove the lamb from the oven and allow it to rest for 4–5 minutes. Meanwhile, sauté the chorizo for 1 minute on each side.

To prepare the dish, slice the lamb and serve it over the beans. Garnish with the clams and chorizo, then drizzle over the gremolata.

Tiramisu

for the sponge
7 eggs
125g caster sugar
50g cocoa powder

for the filling
200g caster sugar
3 egg yolks
500g double cream
500g marscapone

for the espresso liquor
50g sugar
100ml water
3 x 150ml shots of strong espresso coffee
50ml Amaretto
cocoa powder to dust

For the sponge: preheat the oven to 150°C (gas mark 2). Whisk the eggs and sugar on high in a food processor, leaving them for about 6 minutes until the sabayon is stiff. Gently fold in the cocoa powder and smooth the mixture out on to non-stick baking parchment on a baking tray. Bake it in the oven for about 10 minutes, then allow it to cool.

For the filling: put the sugar in a pan and moisten it with a little water (not too much). Put it on the heat and bring it up to 120°C (soft-ball stage). Place the egg yolks in a blender on high speed, add the soft-ball sugar to the eggs and whisk it for about 10 minutes. Once the mixture has cooled, combine the cream and marscapone, pour the sabayon over and gently fold it in. Note: the eggs are cooked from the heat of the boiling sugar.

For the espresso liquor: dissolve the sugar in the water with the espresso and Amaretto, then allow to cool.

To prepare the dish, cut the sponge using a deep metal cutter (I use a piece of sterilised drain-pipe to cut mine). Brush it with the espresso liquor, and layer the discs up with the filling sandwiched in between. Continue this to the desired height, and dust with cocoa powder to serve. Garnish with a simple reduction of espresso and sugar if desired.

Giles Thompson
The Ritz, London

Giles Thompson
The Ritz, London

I have been immersed in the food industry ever since I was born. My father was a farmer and butcher, and my mother was an excellent home cook – an environment that made me determined to become involved in some way.

I was incredibly fortunate to spend nine years training under the brilliant Michel Bourdin at The Connaught, a true master of the techniques and traditions of *haute cuisine*. I worked hard and in 1996 moved to Danesford House, Buckinghamshire, where I achieved two AA rosettes and an RAC restaurant award almost immediately for my style of classical cuisine with a contemporary twist.

I now do my utmost to maintain and uphold the traditions of classical cookery, and believe that it is vital to pass on these skills – not to mention the enthusiasm and dedication they require – to young chefs. I joined The Ritz as Executive Chef in 1997 and am responsible for all menus in the Ritz Restaurant, The Palm Court, the private dining rooms and room service. Presenting a new menu every three months to reflect the best seasonal ingredients and flavours, not to mention creating a '*du jour*' menu featuring a daily selection of seasonal products, is a wonderful culinary challenge. In it I combine traditional and modern styles to present dishes that fulfil our customers' highest expectations. Every dish, however simple, is scrumptious – made of the finest produce and perfectly presented.

Our nine-course Millennium dinner was one of the many high points here, when I believe that every dish and each wine was perfect for the occasion. I try to make a point of remaining calm and level-headed in everything I do, and this magnificent event went a long way towards achieving my ambition of developing meals that complement one of the world's most stunning dining rooms.

I am passionate about food, and hope that you get a taste of The Ritz, London from the dishes that follow.

Giles Thompson
The Ritz, London

Timbale of langoustine, crab and lobster

with watercress sauce

for the sauce
1 bunch of watercress
200ml double cream
50g mayonnaise, readymade
salt and white pepper
squeeze of lemon juice

for the tomato coulis
200g fresh sun-ripened plum
tomatoes, quartered
50g shallots, roughly chopped
25g fresh basil, roughly chopped
100ml dry white wine
100ml water
25g tomato purée

for the timbale
500g Canadian lobster
8 medium langoustines, roughly
diced
200g white crab meat, picked and
roughly chopped
salt and white pepper
1 tsp Dijon mustard
200ml whipping cream
4 leaves of gelatine, softened in a
little water

for the candied zest
1 lemon
10g caster sugar

for the lobster oil
lobster shell, chopped small
500ml olive oil
salt and white pepper

other ingredients
24g oscietre caviar
10g salmon keta
4 sprigs of chervil

For the sauce: remove the leaves from the watercress, reserving the best ones for the garnish. Blend them with a little water to make a purée, slowly add the mayonnaise and double cream, and season with the salt, pepper and lemon juice before passing the sauce through a fine sieve and chilling until needed.

For the tomato coulis: preheat the oven to 200°C (gas mark 6). Combine all the ingredients and then roast them in the oven for 30 minutes, before pushing the tomato mixture through a fine sieve and keeping the coulis warm on one side until needed.

For the timbale: pick and roughly dice the lobster meat, reserving the claws and 4 medallions from the tail. Then mix together the diced lobster, langoustines and crab meat, and season them with salt and pepper. In a separate bowl, dissolve the gelatine in 300ml of your tomato coulis, mix in the mustard and whipping cream, and fold in the lobster mixture, correcting the seasoning with a little more salt and pepper. Then spoon it into four $5^1/_2$ x 5 cm metal rings, and put it in the fridge until needed.

For the candied zest: zest the lemon, and cut the remaining fruit into 4, reserving it for the juice. To remove the bitterness from the zest, place it in a pan with enough water to cover it and bring this to the boil, cooling it under cold running water and repeating the process twice more. Then boil the sugar in a pan with the prepared zest and enough water to cover it until you have a syrupy consistency. Drain it off and reserve the zest until needed.

For the lobster oil: pan-fry the chopped lobster shells for about 5 minutes, then add the olive oil to cover, season with salt and pepper and simmer for 20 minutes. Leave the oil to cool until the shells turn it pink, and drain it off through a fine sieve.

To prepare the dish, arrange the reserved watercress leaves in the centre of the plate with the timbale placed on top. Position the lobster medallion on top of this, finishing with the caviar and sprig of chevil. Diagonally slice half a lobster claw and place this to one side, garnished with the candied lemon zest. Spoon the watercress sauce to the side and garnish with a touch of keta. Drizzle the lobster oil around the edge and serve.

Giles Thompson
The Ritz, London

Seared Devon scallops

with white bean broth

for the broth

100g coco beans

50g onion, peeled and chopped

25g smoked bacon

50g unsalted butter

100ml chicken stock

salt and white pepper

100ml double cream

10ml truffle oil

for the beans

80g broad beans, peeled

40g borlotti beans

40g coco beans

40g flageolet beans

other ingredients

12 scallops

1 tsp olive oil

40g celeriac, cut into fine strips

vegetable oil for deep-frying

truffle oil

4 sprigs of chervil

20g black truffle, cut into fine strips

If any of the beans are not in season, use dried ones and soak them overnight in water.

For the broth: sweat the onion and bacon in 20g of the butter, add the beans and cover them with chicken stock, seasoning and bringing the mixture to the boil. Simmer for about 1 1/2 hours until tender. Remove the bacon, and blitz the beans in a liquidiser with enough cooking liquor to give a purée consistency. Heat the bean purée in a pan with the cream, and bring it to the boil. Add the truffle oil and remaining butter, cut into small pieces. Then froth the broth with a hand blender and adjust the seasoning to taste.

For the beans: cook any dried beans as for the broth but without liquidising. Drain them and allow them to cool.

To prepare the dish, sear the scallops in a hot non-stick pan with a touch of olive oil, and cook for 2 minutes on either side until caramelised on both sides. Deep-fry the celeriac at 160°C until crisp and dry but not brown, and reheat the beans in a little butter and water. Drain the beans and place them in the bottom of a soup plate. Put the scallops in the centre and pour the frothy broth around the edge. Drizzle with the truffle oil, and garnish the top of the scallops with the crispy celeriac and chervil, sprinkling the fine strips of black truffle around (if available).

Giles Thompson
The Ritz, London

Tournedos rossini

for the potato galettes
500g Maris Piper potatoes
10g black truffles, chopped
75g unsalted butter
for the truffle sauce
20g unsalted butter
50g smoked raw ham, diced
75g shallots, peeled and chopped
trimmings from the fillet steaks
1 litre veal stock
20g black truffles, chopped
200ml Madeira wine
salt and white pepper
for the beef
4 x 150g fillet steaks
olive oil
other ingredients
4 x 50g fresh duck liver (foie gras),
sliced
2 slices of thick white bread
10g black winter truffle, thinly
sliced
4 medium asparagus tips

For the potato galettes: preheat the oven to 190°C (gas mark 5). Peel the potatoes, shape them into cylinders then slice them very thinly on a mandolin. Butter four 12cm non-stick ovenproof dishes thoroughly, and place the sliced potato in a circle, with each slice overlapping halfway across the previous slice. Sprinkle them with chopped truffle, then add another layer of potato, then truffle, then finish with potato. Place a knob of butter on to each dish, and put them in the oven for 12 minutes. Remove and drain off any excess butter on kitchen paper.

For the truffle sauce: melt the butter in a heavy-bottomed pan. Add the ham, shallots and beef trimmings, and colour rapidly for a few minutes. Cover with the veal stock and reduce by half.

Sweat off the chopped truffle in a little butter in a separate pan and add the Madeira. Bring it to the boil, add the reduced veal stock, then reduce the mixture to a sauce consistency that coats the back of a spoon. Just before serving, whisk through a little butter and season to taste.

For the beef: preheat the oven to 200°C (gas mark 6). Seal the fillet steaks in a little oil in a hot ovenproof pan, then place them in the oven to cook as required – 3–4 minutes for rare.

To prepare the dish, place the slices of duck liver in a very hot, non-stick pan and cook them until golden brown on both sides. Cut 4 round croûtons out of the bread and pan-fry them in a little olive oil until golden brown. Cut the asparagus tips into about 3cm lengths, cook them quickly in boiling salted water until tender and refresh in iced water.

Take 4 hot plates, and place the potato galette in the centre with the fillet on top. Add the pan-fried croûton on top of that, with the seared duck liver above. Then take the asparagus tips, cut them in half lengthways, reheat and place them on the duck liver. Finally add the slice of truffle and finish with a little sauce around the edge.

Giles Thompson
The Ritz, London

Dark bitter chocolate fondant

for the ganache

50ml double cream

50g dark bitter chocolate, 66% (Valrhona), chopped

for the fondant

100g dark bitter chocolate, 66%

100g unsalted butter

40ml pasteurised egg yolks

100ml pasteurised whole eggs

50g caster sugar

28g plain flour

for the sauce

115ml water

40g dark chocolate

50g caster sugar

40g soft brown sugar

7g cornflour

10g cocoa powder for dusting

For the ganache: bring the cream to the boil, then add the chopped chocolate. Stir until smooth, then spoon the mixture on to a baking tray lined with greaseproof paper to a depth of 1cm. Allow it to cool, and place it in the fridge for about 3 hours until set. Cut it into 1^1/$_2$cm squares.

For the fondant: melt the chocolate in a bain-marie and mix in the butter. Beat together the yolks, whole eggs and the sugar, combine these with the chocolate mix and fold in the flour.

Butter well four 5cm tall, 5.5cm diameter metal rings, and pipe them half-full with the fondant mixture. Add a piece of ganache, and fill the ring up with more fondant mixture until it is to two-thirds full. Store it in the fridge until needed.

For the dark chocolate sauce: bring 90ml water to the boil with the dark chocolate and caster sugar. Mix the soft brown sugar with the remaining water and cornflour in a bowl, then add them to the first mixture and boil them again for about 35 minutes until the sauce thickens. Strain the mixture and allow it to cool.

To prepare the dish, preheat the oven to 220°C (gas mark 7). Cook the fondant for 15 minutes, remove it and place it on a plate, lifting it out of the rings. Surround it with sauce, dust with cocoa powder and serve.

Brian Turner
Turner's

Brian Turner
Turner's

It's still quite strange to me that so many people know my face. But programmes like *Ready, Steady, Cook*, *Food and Drink*, *Out to Lunch* and *Anything You Can Cook* have helped make me into quite a television personality nowadays.

Despite all this, I do spend as much time as possible at Turner's, greeting as many of our customers personally as I can. I opened my restaurant in 1986 after having been lucky enough to work at some of the most prestigious hotels and restaurants in Europe. My early mentor was the food writer and broadcaster, the late Michael Smith, and my first real job was at Simpson's in the Strand with Richard Shepherd (founder of Langan's Brasserie). After two years I followed Richard to The Savoy Grill, working under Louis Virot, and then decided to develop my skills and understanding of classical cuisine at Beau Rivage Palace in Lausanne, Switzerland.

I returned to England and worked at Claridges until 1971, when I once more teamed up with Richard – this time at the Michelin-starred Capital Hotel, Knightsbridge, and this time becoming Chef de Cuisine, a role I fulfilled for nine years. It was an exciting time. Many well-known chefs worked for me there, Gary Rhodes and Sean Hill among them – both of whom now have their own Michelin stars. And I was also responsible for the launch of both The Greenhouse in Mayfair and the Metro Wine Bar in Basil Street, becoming Executive Chef of both.

For all that, though, Turner's in Walton Street, Knightsbridge, is where my heart is. The personal attention devoted to both the food and our guests immediately attracted a regular clientele of local residents, as well as a devoted international following. In a very real sense, it set new standards among the British chef-owned restaurants that are now a feature of dining out in London. So, although the many awards I have won over the years are a bonus and the various engagements at leading hotels around the world great fun, I always come back to Turner's with a huge sense of pride and satisfaction.

Smoked salmon and prawn slice

with a chilli lime dressing

8 slices of smoked salmon
110g Philadelphia cheese
8 giant Mediterranean prawns, 4 whole and 4 finely chopped
1 tbsp vinaigrette, ready-made
1 tbsp chives, chopped
salt and white pepper

for the dressing
1 large red chilli, finely chopped
zest of 1 lime
juice of 1 lime
2 tbsp soy sauce
4 tbsp olive oil
1 clove of garlic, peeled and crushed
1 tsp caster sugar
1 tbsp chopped parsley
12 whole chives

Cut out eight 5cm circles from the smoked salmon and chop up the rest of it. Mix the chopped salmon with the cheese and prawns, add the vinaigrette, chopped chives and salt and pepper and leave to one side. Lay 1 circle of salmon in the bottom of a ring mould. Spoon the mixture on top, flatten it down, lay a second circle of salmon on top and press flat.

For the dressing: mix the chilli with the lime zest, and add the lime juice, soy sauce and olive oil. Add the garlic, sugar and parsley, and season to taste.

To serve, carefully remove the salmon from the mould and lay it in the centre of a plate. Drizzle the sauce around, using the whole chives to decorate.

Tower of scallops and smoked haddock

in a champagne butter sauce

2 tomatoes, deseeded and diced
1 shallot, peeled and chopped
10g unsalted butter
1 clove of garlic, crushed
100ml olive oil
175g smoked haddock, sliced
8 scallops, sliced
salt and white pepper
for the sauce
2 shallots, peeled and chopped
1 glass of dry white wine
1 glass of champagne
1 tbsp white wine vinegar
300ml fish stock
150ml double cream
175g unsalted butter
salt and white pepper
1 tbsp chopped chives
for the garnish
2 leeks, finely chopped
10g unsalted butter
100ml double cream
4–5 new potatoes per person

Sweat off the tomato and shallot in a little butter for 3 minutes and set them aside to cool. Mix together the garlic and olive oil and allow them to gently infuse for 5–10 minutes. Lay slices of haddock in the base of four 7cm cooking rings, add a little of the garlic oil to each, then top with slices of scallop. Season, add a little of the tomato and shallot mixture, and repeat the layering, finishing with a layer of scallop.

Cut out four 8^1/$_2$cm squares of greaseproof paper or foil. Sit each cooking ring in a steamer over a saucepan with a little simmering water in the base, the greaseproof paper being placed above and below each ring to protect the fish from the heat. Place the lid on the steamer then steam the scallop and haddock rings for around 6 minutes.

For the sauce: place the shallots in a pan, add the wine, champagne, white wine vinegar and fish stock, and simmer to reduce the liquid by half. Add the double cream and reduce the liquid by one-third. Slowly beat in the butter, season to taste, and add the chives. Leave to infuse on the side of the stove.

To prepare the dish, sauté the leeks in a little butter, then add the cream. Boil the new potatoes. Remove the cooking rings from the steamer and dry them off. To serve, place the scallop and haddock towers on a bed of creamed leeks and new potatoes and pour the sauce over.

Breast and confit leg of duck

4 large legs of duck
2 tbsp Malden sea salt
2 bay leaves, chopped
2 sprigs of fresh thyme, rubbed
1 whole garlic head
1 onion, roughly diced
1 carrot, roughly diced
1 litre melted duck fat
4 duck breasts

for the Madeira sauce

2 shallots, peeled and chopped
75g unsalted butter
1 glass Madeira – rich bual
1 glass dry white wine
300ml reduced veal stock

For best results, you need to begin preparing this dish a couple of days in advance. Make sure the duck legs are free of quills and wax. Lay them on a baking tray, and sprinkle them with the sea salt, bay leaves and thyme. Cut the garlic head in half, pile the duck legs around, and cover with clingfilm. Leave to marinate for 24 hours, then wash off the herbs and pat dry.

Preheat the oven to 140°C (gas mark 1). Lay the marinated legs in a deep, heavy-based pot and add the onion, carrot and remaining garlic. Cover with melted duck fat, put the lid on and cook in the oven for 2–3 hours until the meat is ready to fall off the bone. Make sure the fat does not boil. When cooked, take the legs out and leave them to cool, then decant the duck legs into a clean bowl. Strain the fat through a fine chinois over the duck legs and refrigerate for 2 days. (They will keep like this for ages if covered with the fat.)

For the Madeira sauce: sweat off the shallots in 25g of the butter; do not allow them to colour. Add the Madeira and white wine and reduce by two-thirds. Add the reduced veal stock and bring to the boil, simmering for 3–5 minutes. Slowly add the remaining butter, swirling it all the time.

To prepare the dish, preheat the oven to 210°C (gas mark 7). Remove the fat from the duck legs. Heat up an ovenproof frying pan, then place the duck breasts in it flesh-side down for 2 minutes. Turn them over, add the duck legs skin-side down, and put the pan in the oven for 10 minutes until hot all the way through. Take them out and drain on kitchen paper.

Whisk the sauce and serve the duck, skin-side up, with the sauce – perhaps on top of a hotpot potato with mangetout, as shown here.

Iced cherry parfait

with a griottine cherry compote

for the parfait
50ml water
75g sugar
2 egg yolks
120g frozen cherries
50g griottine cherries
25ml liquor from cherries
125ml double cream

for the compote
450g frozen cherries
200g griottine cherries
100ml liquor from cherries
200g caster sugar

For the parfait: boil up the water and sugar to produce a stock syrup, then set it aside until warm. Whisk the egg yolks in a blender, then add the warmed syrup and whisk up the sabayon. Boil the cherries and liquor for 3–4 minutes, then blend in a food processor. Carefully fold a quarter of the cherry mixture into the sabayon and then a quarter of the cream. Repeat until all the cherry mixture and cream have been incorporated. Pour into a terrine mould lined with clingfilm and freeze overnight.

For the compote: place all the ingredients in a pan and simmer for 8–10 minutes. Remove the cherries, keeping them on one side, and reduce the liquor to leave a syrup that coats the back of a spoon. Allow this to cool and then add to the cherries. Chill until required.

To serve, place the compote on a plate, top with three triangles of parfait and drizzle a little syrup around the edge.

Annie Wayte
Nicole's

Annie Wayte
Nicole's

I knew from a very early age that I wanted to spend lots of time in the kitchen. I remember making marzipan sweets at the age of three with my grandmother, and by the age of nine I was dreaming of running my own cookery school.

For me, it was food or nothing and I decided to get tough. So I landed my first position by knocking on the back door of London's Hilton Hotel and talking my way into a brigade of 130 chefs. But after a few years of working in upscale hotels, I knew that I had to seek out places where I could cook on a more intimate scale and use the premium ingredients that have become both my passion and my signature.

Designer Nicole Farhi's search for a chef to develop the menu for her namesake restaurant came just as I felt ready to head up a kitchen of my own. In 1994 we opened Nicole's, a restaurant that proved so successful that just five years later I opened a branch in New York.

I now divide my time between the two cities, cooking, planning menus and training staff at both locations. We rely on fresh, seasonal produce, in prime condition and either organic or bought from small farms. So, for example, when I receive tomatoes in late August, I create a dish that emphasises their deliciousness. Nothing complicated, nothing that will cloud their identity. Simple, bold food in a Mediterranean/modern European style is what we offer – inspired by the family-run restaurants that I track down on my travels, but reinterpreted in the unique Nicole's way.

And who knows? Maybe the doors of The Annie Wayte Cookery School will open one day.

Buffalo mozzarella, fennel and toasted almond salad

with lemon and mint dressing

170g salad leaves, trimmed and washed

1 bulb of fennel, tough outer layer removed

250g buffalo mozzarella

80g whole almonds, blanched and toasted

1 tbsp chives, cut into small batons

30g wild wood sorrel (optional)

for the dressing

6 tbsp extra virgin olive oil

4 tbsp lemon juice

zest of 1 lemon

$1/4$ tsp Dijon mustard

$1/4$ tsp garlic, minced

1 tsp fresh mint leaves, chopped

1 pinch of salt and black pepper

8 nasturtium flowers (optional garnish)

Divide the salad leaves equally between 4 serving plates. Slice the fennel finely into rings, and cut the mozzarella into 8 pieces, arranging both over the salad. Scatter the toasted almonds, chives and wild wood sorrel over the top.

For the dressing: place all the dressing ingredients in a bowl and whisk them together until the dressing has emulsified. Taste and adjust the seasoning.

To serve, drizzle the dressing over the salad, and garnish it with the nasturtium flowers.

Grilled tuna

with braised borlotti beans, wilted spinach, and tomato and basil relish

4 x 240g tuna loin fillets
salt and black pepper to taste
for the relish
480g fresh tomatoes
salt and black pepper
3 tbsp extra virgin olive oil
1 clove of garlic, peeled and minced
1 small red chilli, finely chopped
1 small red onion, peeled and finely diced
30g sun-dried tomatoes, sliced into thin strips
1 small bunch green basil, picked and washed
1 small bunch purple basil, picked and washed
for the borlotti beans
880g fresh borlotti beans, cooked plus 8 tbsp reserved cooking liquor (use tinned drained borlotti beans if fresh are unavailable, with 8 tbsp water)
1 clove of garlic, peeled and minced
2 tbsp extra virgin olive oil
2 medium leeks, trimmed and sliced on an angle
200g spinach leaves, trimmed and washed

For the relish: score the skin of each tomato and blanch in boiling water for 10 seconds. Remove and plunge into ice-cold water until each tomato is chilled. Drain them and peel off the skins, discarding these. Cut the tomatoes into quarters, remove the tomato seeds with a small vegetable knife and discard them. Place the tomato flesh into a bowl and season with salt and pepper. Add the extra virgin olive oil, minced garlic, chopped chilli and chopped red onion and stir well to ensure the tomatoes are evenly coated. Allow them to macerate for approximately 20 minutes or until they become juicy. (The amount of time this takes will depend upon the quality of the tomatoes: if the tomatoes are ripe they should start to form a pool of tasty juices in the bottom of the bowl.) Add the strips of sun-dried tomato, and finally toss the basil leaves into the relish.

For the borlotti beans: place the borlotti beans in a saucepan with the reserved cooking liquor, minced garlic, olive oil and salt and pepper over a medium heat until the borlotti beans are hot. Add the leeks and gently simmer for approximately 4 minutes until they start to soften. Then add the spinach leaves, gently wilting them over a low heat for about a minute. Keep these warm until required.

For the tuna: preheat the charcoal grill – or griddle pan, sauté pan or barbecue, if not available. Season the tuna steaks with salt and pepper and smear the surface of each one with a small amount of olive oil to prevent them from sticking on the grill. Cook them to your liking. If you prefer your tuna steak rare, I would suggest you grill it for approximately 2–3 minutes on each side, depending on the thickness of the steaks.

When the tuna is cooked, divide the beans into 4 serving bowls and place the tuna on top. Garnish each plate with a spoonful of tomato and basil relish and serve.

4 ripe figs
1 tbsp soft brown sugar
zest of 1 orange
2 tbsp fig balsamic vinegar
(available from good delicatessens)

for the roasted onions

2 medium red onions, peeled and
cut into rings
1 bunch of spring onions, trimmed
1 bunch of grelot onions, trimmed
(if unavailable, use pickling onions,
peeled)
2 tbsp extra virgin olive oil
rosemary spears from 4 rosemary
sticks (reserve sticks for the
garnish)
salt and black pepper

for the duck

4 duck breasts, trimmed and
scored
salt and black pepper

for the sauce

300ml fresh duck stock (use
chicken stock if duck not available)
zest of 1 orange
1 star anise
90ml dry white wine
1 clove of garlic, peeled
2 tbsp walnut oil
splash of fig balsamic vinegar
salt and black pepper

for the garnish

4 slices of pancetta
4 x 2cm cubed bread croûtons
(use soured dough bread or plain
white bread, crusts removed)
4 x 25g duck liver, trimmed
4 fresh sage leaves
4 sticks of rosemary (reserved)
120g red/green mustard leaves,
trimmed and washed

Pan-fried duck breast

with figs, roasted onions, red mustard leaves and fig
balsamic dressing

Slice each fig in half and place in a mixing bowl. Add the soft brown
sugar, orange zest and fig balsamic vinegar, toss the ingredients together
and allow to macerate for at least 1 hour.

For the roasted onion: about half an hour after macerating the figs,
preheat the oven to 200°C (gas mark 6). Place the different varieties of
onion in a thick-bottomed dish, and toss them with the olive oil and
rosemary spears. (Don't forget to retain the rosemary sticks for the
garnish!) Season the onions with salt and pepper and place them in the
oven for approximately 25 minutes or until the onions are golden brown
and tender. Approximately 5 minutes before the onions are cooked, drain
the figs from their marinade and add them to the onions.

For the duck: preheat a frying pan large enough to fit the 4 breasts.
Season each and place them skin-side down in the pan. Gently cook for
about 4 minutes until the skin turns golden brown and becomes crispy.
Once you have achieved this, turn the breasts over and continue to cook
for about 5 minutes more. This will give you a medium cooked breast. If
you prefer it cooked without visible blood, I would suggest you leave it
for about 8 minutes or until it feels firm to the touch. Remove them from
the pan and allow to rest for approximately 8 minutes.

For the sauce: place the duck stock in a pan with the orange zest, star anise,
white wine and garlic. Bring to the boil, then lower the heat and simmer until
the stock has reduced by half. Remove it from the stove and pass through
a fine sieve, discarding the contents left in the sieve. Whisk in the walnut oil
with the fig balsamic, and season with salt and pepper. Taste and adjust the
sauce with the fig balsamic and walnut oil to your liking.

For the garnish: lay a slice of pancetta on to your work surface. Place the
bread croûton in the middle, with a duck liver and sage leaf on top. Take
each end of the pancetta and wrap it around the edge. Using the
rosemary stick as a skewer, thread it through the croûton and secure it
together, repeating this with the other 3 croûtons. When the skewers are
assembled, gently fry them in the same frying pan as the duck breasts
while they are resting. Cook for about 3 minutes on each side or until the
pancetta is golden brown and the livers are cooked to your liking.

To prepare the dish, arrange the mustard leaves over 4 serving dishes
and divide the onions and figs between each plate. Slice the duck breasts
and arrange these over the top. Place the duck liver garnish on the top.
Warm the sauce gently in a saucepan over a low heat, stirring well, then
drizzle over each dish and serve.

Baked almond peaches

with clotted cream and almond cookies

for the almond cream
75g unsalted butter
75g icing sugar
2 eggs
125g ground almonds
zest of 1 lemon
20g flour

for the peaches
4 peaches, halved and stoned
30g flaked almonds
4 tbsp clotted cream to serve

for the almond biscuits
150g chopped almonds, toasted
250g caster sugar
160g flour
1/4 tsp baking powder
1 egg
1/2 tsp lemon juice

For the almond cream: let the butter soften at room temperature, then beat it for 1–2 minutes with a wooden spoon until creamy. Gradually beat in the icing sugar and continue beating vigorously for 3–5 minutes; the mixture will become creamy and fluffy, and almost double in volume. Add the eggs one by one, beating well after each addition, then stir in the ground almonds, flour and lemon zest.

For the peaches: preheat the oven to 170°C (gas mark 3), and place the peach halves in a gratin dish. Using either a teaspoon or a piping bag, put almond cream into each peach cavity, sprinkle the flaked almonds over the top and bake for about 20 minutes or until the almond cream has risen and turned golden brown.

For the almond biscuits: preheat the oven to 170°C (gas mark 3). Mix all the ingredients together and spoon them on to a baking tray lined with parchment paper. Bake in the oven for about 8 minutes or until the biscuits are golden brown. Allow them to cool on a wire rack.

Serve the peach halves in serving bowls with a scoop of clotted cream and almond biscuits.

Contributors

Bar Zaika Bazaar
2a Pond Place
London SW3 6QU
Tel: 0207 584 6655

The People's Palace
Level 3
Royal Festival Hall
Southbank
London SE1 8XX
Tel: 0207 928 9999

John Burton-Race Restaurant
The Landmark Hotel
222 Marylebone Road
London NW1 6JQ
Tel: 0207 631 8230

The Neal Street Restaurant
26 Neal Street
London WC2H 9QW
Tel: 0207 836 8368

Mirabelle
56 Curzon Street
London W1J 8PA
Tel: 0207 499 4636

Sonny's
94 Church Road
London SW13 0DQ
Tel: 0208 748 0393

Aubergine
11 Park Walk
London SW10 0AG
Tel: 0207 352 3449

Orrery
55 Marylebone High Street
London W1M 3AE
Tel: 0207 616 8000

The Conservatory
The Lanesborough
Hyde Park Corner
London SW1X 7TA
Tel: 0207 333 7254

St John
26 St John Street
London EC1M 4AY
Tel: 0207 512 0848

Searcy's at the Barbican
Level 2
Barbican Centre
Silk Street
London EC2Y 8DS
Tel: 0207 588 3008

The Greenhouse
27A Hay's Mews
London W1X 7RJ
Tel: 0207 499 3314

Teatro
93–107 Shaftesbury Avenue
London W1D 6DY
Tel: 0207 494 3040

Quo Vadis
26–29 Dean Street
London W1V 6LL
Tel: 0207 437 9585

The Ritz, London
150 Piccadilly
London W1V 9DG
Tel: 0207 300 2370

Turner's
89 Walton Street
London SW3 2HP
Tel: 0207 584 6711

Nicole's
158 New Bond Street
London W1Y 9PA
Tel: 0207 499 8408

Index